The World is NOT Enough

OR, CAN MOVIES SAVE THE WORLD?

I was watching the film *Jupiter Ascending* the way it was meant to be seen: via premium streaming service. It had something to do with Channing Tatum, rocket-powered rollerblades, Eddie Redmayne screaming while wearing a shower curtain, Sean Bean pretending to be half bee, and a breathless tussle to ensure the future of planet Earth. It was fun. But there was something odd about the experience, beyond the bee acting. This is a film in which, like so many before it, the fate of mankind hangs in the balance. Yet it was hard to suppress the thought: would it be so bad if we were all compacted and transformed into space crystals and ingested by intergalactic royalty to extend their lives? Maybe it's what we deserve.

On the occasion of our 75th issue, and inspired by the mild apocalyptic rumblings at time of production, we wanted to do something different. The question posed by this issue is: can movies save the world? Does art have the power to change a mind or alter a perception? When all else fails, how do we appeal to a person's sense of justice?

The reality is, we can never know if movies have the power to smash through the subconscious and provoke in the viewer an impulse to alter his or her life – to take action where it otherwise might not have been taken. Maybe that's why cinema holds the appeal it does; we can watch, safe in the knowledge that it won't fundamentally change who we are. As propaganda, cinema is often transparent. Humans are built with psychological checks and balances which help us acknowledge the differences between reality and fiction.

In reality, movies tend to provoke private, passive epiphanies which spark a cyclical desire to watch more movies. That's why we talk about movies as "product" – they are fed to us as much as we consume them. Maybe the drama associated with collective death from above – the plotline of most fiction features – is softened by the fact that consuming cinema now is so often a case of watching a person in a coloured leotard hitting another person in a coloured leotard in the name of humanity's preservation. Every single week. Without fail.

But what if movies themselves were the superheroes? What if they had the power to swoop in and save everything just before the ticking clock shifts between one and zero? Secretly we're not really asking whether movies can save the world. Let's, for the sake of argument, say that they can, and ask, if you could save the world with movies, then what would you actually wield that power? Consider the question we sent out to a number of friends, contributors and persons of high artistic repute on the opposite page.

We realise it's an unlikely hypothetical scenario. Especially as it has been well documented that Donald Trump's most high profile interactions with cinema are a contractually obliged cameo in *Home Alone 2: Lost in New York*, and fast-forwarding through *Bloodsport* (see page 30) while gliding on a golden jet. Plus, it's a scenario which does fan the flames of global anxiety for the sake of a playful thought experiment. There is a hyperbolic undertow to the idea that the world is in such a bad state that it needs saving. The people at the top are perhaps more antagonistic, hubristic, power hungry and volatile than they have been in a good long while, but we're under no delusions that things have probably been worse.

Thinking about movies this way might prize the medium's thematic over its aesthetic properties, but responders to this brief have embraced aesthetics as way to articulate a theme. Over the ensuing pages, we offer a newly curated selection of films, each intended as last line of defence against a world going wrong. There are no top tens or multiple choices. Each contributor has to go all-in on a single film. Some might see this as reductive – a cruel game which strips back the essential poetics of the medium – but that's not the case. Many have deduced that the most penetrating insights are often born from the germ of potent visuals and carefully calibrated storytelling.

Scanning over the films that have been chosen, some broad themes emerge. Nuclear anxiety appears high on people's list of world-saving priorities, and there is a desire to show these people the build-up and fall-out of such drastic action. Some believe that this is a futile exercise and have selected punishingly long films in an attempt to keep this audience from getting up to further mischief. Others have taken the tack that the only way to forge a meaningful connection with this type of audience is to treat them to a double dose of cinematic joy in an attempt to convince them that, y'know, life can be beautiful.

So here are the movies which, we guarantee you, will save the world. Each contributor has selected a film and written a short note explaining their choice. As these films have all been presumed to posses qualities which might coax humanity back from the ledge, maybe that would make them some of the best ever made. It's certainly not a traditional selection of tried-and-tested canonical classics – more a list of works that have touched a personal nerve. Watch them all, and then rewatch *Jupiter Ascending* in the hope that future of the world can be enough once more.

David Jenkins

Brief

Dear friend,

We contact you on the occasion of the 75th issue of Little White Lies.
We are working on a project and we'd love to have you involved. We are
looking at the subject of whether movies can save the world.
Context: the world is fucked.
If you had the most politically influential people in the world – politicians, CEOs,
philanthropists, etc – as a captive audience in a cinema, what movie would you screen
to them and why? All we would like is the name of the movie and your justification.
Please interpret this question as you like. The aim of this feature is to produce an
alternative canon of films, each hand-selected by a diverse array of collaborators.

Thanks

David Jenkins
Editor, LWLies

ESTEEMED Respondents

Lenny Abrahamson	Phil Concannon	David Jenkins	Mike McCahill	Roxanne Sancto
Mark Adams	Stephen Cone	Timothy George Kelly	Katherine McLaughlin	Michael Sheen
Babak Anvari	Laia Costa	Brodie Lancaster	Tuppence Middleton	Josh Slater-Williams
Mark Asch	Adam Lee Davies	Joe Lawlor	Sophie Monks Kaufman	Michael Smiley
JA Bayona	Guillermo Del Toro	Elena Lazic	Adam Nayman	Justine Smith
Abby Bender	Hope Dickson Leach	Manuela Lazic	Jarod Neece	Matt Thrift
Anton Bitel	Ella Donald	Michael Leader	Christina Newland	Colin Trevorrow
Laurène Boglio	Emma Fraser	Guy Lodge	Ben Nicholson	Matt Turner
Edith Bowman	Marya E Gates	Kim Longinotto	Charlie Phillips	Beth Webb
Charles Bramesco	Caroline Golum	James Luxford	Gina Prince-Blythewood	Hannah Woodhead
Holly Brockwell	Glenn Heath Jr.	Christine Malloy	Laurie Rose	Adam Woodward
Efe Cakarel	Thomas Hobbs	Alicia Malone	Benny Safdie	
Michelle Carey	Tom Huddleston	Ian Mantgani	Josh Safdie	
Jaime Christley	Pamela Hutchinson	Penny Martin	Carol Salter	

IF YOU HAD THE MOST IMPORTANT AND INFLUENTIAL PEOPLE IN THE WORLD AS A CAPTIVE AUDIENCE, WHICH MOVIE WOULD YOU SCREEN TO THEM AND WHY?

KEY TO COMMON THEMES

 Apocalyptic anxiety

 Dark Tech

 Fascist tendencies

 Money troubles

 Visions of happiness

 Existential angst

 Cine-punishment

 Spiritual contentment

 Tough Love

 Smash the system

Directed by Armando Iannucci, 2017
Words by Mike McCahill, Illustration
by Pepa Prieto Puy, Type by Oliver Stafford

THE DEATH OF STALIN

Politics as farce, politics as skullduggery and politics as death.

It strikes me, looking at our present dystopian logjam, that the problem is one of across-the-board entrenchment. We've grown suspicious of giving valuable time to anything that doesn't appear to conform to our pre-established beliefs; one can no more visualise Bernie Sanders sitting down with 'The Fountainhead' than one can Theresa May running in from the wheatfields to catch up with *I, Daniel Blake*. And can you imagine Vladimir Putin being won over by *Paddington*? 'This is not a Russian bear.' Increasingly there is an assumption that if it's not made by and for Us, then it can only be for Them.

Reaching past *Lincoln*, Steven Spielberg's never-more-timely thesis on the need for the diplomatic communication that shapes leaders and pushes things forward, I'm going to defy Mr Putin and show Armando Iannucci's *The Death of Stalin*, which promises a measure of scholarly, BBC Films-backed respectability – I can see Jacob Rees-Mogg rolling his eyes already – but develops into several things at once. A breakneck farce; a tremendous acting showcase; an acknowledgement that isms of any shade are two-thirds of the way towards schism; and, at the last, a sonofabitch warning from history

of where clinging blindly to these dogmas carries us: towards obscuring clouds of smoke and ashes, people disappearing off the face of the planet. The very opposite of political representation ◎

Mike is a freelance writer and broadcaster.

Directed by Jacques Tati, 1953, Words by Mark Adams, Illustration by Pepa Prieto Puy, Type by Oliver Stafford

LES VACANCES DE MONSIEUR HULOT

Hapless Hulot's hijinks by the sea delivers a pure shot of screwball satisfaction.

Can a film save the world? Highly unlikely. But a few films can amuse the world; inspire the world with their compassion while also poking fun at social order and puncture all that is overly self-important. A film like *Les Vacances de Monsieur Hulot* (or *Monsieur Hulot's Holiday*, as it was released in English), a gentle delight that mocks the pompous, the petty and the dilettantes and questions reliance on technology but without aggression or bitterness. Almost silent, it works for any audience and blends physical humour with

astute lampooning of plenty of serious targets. Ultimately it calls for warmth, affection and compassion... which can never be a bad thing ◎

Mark is Artistic Director of the Edinburgh International Film Festival, which takes place from Wednesday 20 June to Sunday 1 July, 2018. For more info visit edfilmfest.org.uk

UNDER THE SKIN

Directed by Jonathan Glazer	Words by Adam Lee Davies	
2013	Illustration by Pepa Prieto Puy	Type by Oliver Stafford

In which a celestial Scarlett Johansson preys upon unsuspecting Scotsmen.

Once I was silver, now I am a fern. Conceived in a star, gestated beneath a mountain, I was born at the tip of a Peruvian mining axe and for a hundred years enjoyed life as a brooch, before being beaten into a goblet. Gemstones glittered around me as I watched Pizarro murdered and his conquistadors scatter for home. I was briefly a ring on the hand of King Ferdinand of Spain before being stolen by a desperate courtesan and used to buy passage on a Portuguese caravel set for the Spice Islands. But the ship's captain was a sick fool and abandoned his cargo and crew for the madam of a Dandong brothel, and so it was that I was melted and moulded into a gleaming silver sex toy of fanciful design and energetic usage along the coast of China.

I was occasionally mistaken for an idol, once used to cudgel a lemur to death, and eventually made my way to Guangzhou, where I felt the hot coals of the smithy's furnace once again. I was a Buddha, a hair pin, a spoon. I travelled to San Francisco as a pair of spectacle frames that saw the Union and the Central railheads meet at Promontory Summit in the Utah Territory. Then I was the molar of a famous vaudevillian who once entertained Lincoln himself before straitened circumstances forced my owner to pawn me to a gunsmith, who laid me into the handle of a Colt Walker pistol - a thundering great heirloom that would one day be lost during the Normandy landings.

Found and taken to England, I cut a murderous swathe through London's gangland before becoming too hot to handle and thus thrown into a landfill. Mechanically reclaimed and shipped to the Kodak factory in Harrow I was compounded with iodine, suspended in a strip of gelatin and placed into a large black film canister. Eventually I was transported to Scotland and exposed to light through the lens of a movie camera, which is when I became a fern behind Scarlett Johansson's left ear. Now I sit mouldering in the storeroom of a failing Glasgow art-house cinema. Once I was silver, now I am a fern. I wonder what I will become next ◎

Adam is a freelance film writer. He was once called a 'naughty boy' by Peter Fonda.

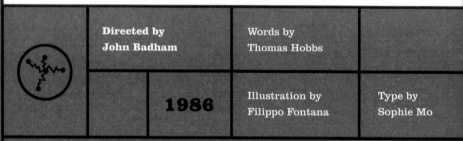

SHORT CIRCUIT

Directed by **John Badham**	Words by **Thomas Hobbs**	
1986	Illustration by **Filippo Fontana**	Type by **Sophie Mo**

Lightning strikes and a hepcat robot with a heart of gold is born.

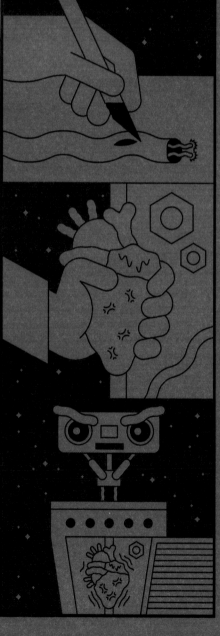

In the surface, 1986's *Short Circuit* feels like a lackadaisical attempt to make the robot equivalent of *E.T.* Look a little deeper and it boldly shows viewers how artificial intelligence can be a force for good, subverting Hollywood's lazy obsession with turning robots into sex slaves and soulless killing machines. *Short Circuit* opens at NOVA Laboratories, a shady research firm that boasts of creating five new military robots capable of blowing Moscow to smithereens. However, by good fortune, robot No. 5 is struck by lightning and malfunctions, which results in its escape from the laboratory and the start of its quest for knowledge.

When it encounters hippie farmer Stephanie (Ally Sheedy), No. 5 repeatedly asks her for 'input', which it is given in the form of encyclopedias, novels and TV. Subsequently, No. 5 develops a profound love for animals, humans and even *Saturday Night Fever* dance moves. Now, according to the late Professor Stephen Hawking: "We cannot quite predict what will happen if a machine exceeds our intelligence. We could conceivably be destroyed by it." I would like to call bullshit on this pessimistic Kubrickian reading of AI, with *Short Circuit*'s No. 5 cinematic proof that if intelligent synthetic lifeforms are treated with love, compassion and knowledge, then they can develop a humanity that isn't dangerous.

By the end of *Short Circuit*, No. 5 develops consciousness and decides it would like to be called Johnny 5. If you forget the fact he looks like a walking VHS machine, then our little metal boy carries an important message: if we teach robots the right things, then their potential for good is endless. *Short Circuit* suggests that if we offer artificial intelligence freedom rather than slavery then the world can be filled with Johnny 5s rather than HAL 9000s ◉

Thomas is a freelance journalist, who actually loves Mother!

No actual grapes, but plenty of wrath.

Grab 'em by the heartstrings: John Ford's adaptation of John Steinbeck's novel offers, in essence, a simple, honest and intensely emotional defence of socialism. Employing every trick in the Hollywood playbook, it aims to sell us the idea that everyone deserves a break, and if we all work together we can make this weary old world a better place for all. Subtle it ain't; truthful it most assuredly is.

Tom Huddleston is a film writer and author of the books 'The Waking World' and 'Star Wars: Adventures in Wild Space'.

Directed by John Ford, 1940
Words by Tom Huddleston, Type by Sophie Mo

An inspirational tale of taking on authority in search of basic human rights.

It might have been easier to choose one of the many amazing documentaries that show us both the horrors and the wonders that humans have wrought on this planet, but as a believer in the power of fiction, I've gone for a drama. (After all, if we don't have filmmakers with strongly held beliefs, this whole enterprise is pointless). Ken Loach's *Ladybird, Ladybird* changed my life. It made me want to be a filmmaker; helped me to understand how the political affects the personal, how relationships and personalities are complex and how desperately we need a society based on love. It's a devastating, heartbreaking film and anyone with any power needs to see it and, most of all, learn to feel the impact of their decisions

Hope Dickson Leach is the writer/director of The Levelling.

Directed by Ken Loach, 1994
Words by Hope Dickson Leach, Type by Laurène Boglio

Directed by Dee Rees, 2011
Words by Marya E Gates, Type by Laurène Boglio

A young black girl attempts to define her own identity.

I would screen *Pariah* by Dee Rees. It's a moving portrait of a young, artistic, queer black girl who comes of age, gets her heart broken, comes out to her family and finds the strength to live her truth and reach for her own happiness above everything else. When I think of strong women in film, Alike (Adepero Oduye) is the first character that comes to mind

Marya works in social media by day and consumes and critiques culture by night.

Directed by Jafar Panahi, 1997
Words by Benny and Josh Safdie, Type by Laurène Boglio

An innovative Iranian fable about a young girl attempting to get home which folds in on itself.

"As a constant reminder that you can't make shit up."

The Safdie brothers are the filmmakers behind the excellent Good Time, Heaven Knows What, *and more...*

Born in Flames

A dose of feminist afrofuturism to dazzle the senses.

Leaders shall observe radicalism in form as well as content, and this is the afrofuturist-feminist-punk bonfire to make it happen. A film packed full of ideas about resistance, revolution and freedom, and with a killer soundtrack. Leaders will bask in its pleasures and rethink everything they have thought. Behold Honey's opening monologue: "For we have stood on the promises, far too long now, that we can all be equal under cover of a social democracy, where the rich get richer and the poor just wait on their dreams"

Michelle Carey is artistic director of the Melbourne. International Film Festival (for the last time this year).

Directed by Lizzie Borden, 1983
Words by Michelle Carey, Type by Laurène Boglio

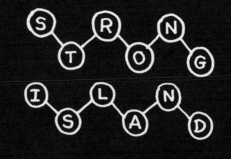

A stirring portrait of how convicts tap into their emotions.

So for the important people, I'd show them the documentary *Strong Island* because they need to hear from people they pretend don't exist or aren't worthy of hearing – a black perspective, a trans perspective, a lower income perspective. And I want them to feel some empathy which seems to be drummed out of you once you become powerful – there aren't many more empathic experiences than being immersed in this film. It also might benefit them to understand that documentaries can be works of art in case they fancy thinking about how culture can be both powerful and beautiful – if they understood that we might have a more compassionate and thoughtful world

Charlie is head of documentaries at the Guardian.

Directed by Yance Ford, 2017
Words by Charlie Phillips, Type by Laurène Boglio

One of the greatest – and darkest – Spanish films ever made.

The Executioner (El Verdugo) from Luis García Berlanga is my bet. It is an overwhelming condemnation of the death penalty. The film is a miracle: a comedy about the death penalty made during Franco's fierce Spanish dictatorship. The final shot shows two terrified men, one condemned to death and the other his executioner, both dragged away to find themselves sharing a terrible destiny. It is undoubtedly one of the most terrifying images cinema has ever produced

JA Bayona is the director of A Monster Calls, The Impossible *and* Jurassic World: Fallen Kingdom *which is released on 6 June, 2018.*

Directed by Luis García Berlanga, 1963
Words by JA Bayona, Type by Laurène Boglio

Positivity radiates from this documentary about tackling climate change.

I cried a lot and decided to start growing brussels sprouts. Think of what it could do for the leaders of the world.

Laurène is art director of Little White Lies.

Directed by Cyril Dion, Mélanie Laurent, 2015
Words and Type by Laurène Boglio

ACADEMY AWARD® NOMINEE 2018
BEST ANIMATED FEATURE FILM

★★★★
TIME OUT

★★★★
THE SKINNY

FROM THE CREATORS OF THE ACADEMY AWARD® - NOMINATED
THE SECRET OF KELLS & SONG OF THE SEA
AND EXECUTIVE PRODUCER
ANGELINA JOLIE

★★★★
LITTLE WHITE LIES

"A RICHLY ANIMATED JEWEL"
★★★★
MATTHEW ANDERSON, CINEVUE

★★★★
TOTAL FILM

THE
Breadwinner

A FILM BY
NORA TWOMEY

12A

IN CINEMAS MAY 25

FIORUCCI MADE ME HARDCORE

Directed by **Mark Leckey**	Words by **Matt Turner**
1999	llustration by **Allison Filice**	Type by **Simon Hayes**

Dance! Dance! Dance!

Mark Leckey's *Fiorucci Made Me Hardcore* starts with a spectral, grain-laden blue skyline. Surreal but serene, this scene sets the tone for the film, a chronological collage covering three decades of UK dance culture that connects northern soul to acid house and hardcore. A peculiar, exuberant film, it is at once nostalgic and euphoric; a reverie for ephemeral counterculture and its increasingly vulnerable position within contemporary society.

Meshing together found footage in intuitive, associative montage, Leckey charts dance spaces across various eras, tracking the changes in dress, dance and drug of choice. A mesmeric soundtrack of atrophied rave snippets, echoing voices and dancefloor field recordings accompanies the visuals. Across time, isolated individuals become a single body, blurry edits create a mutating mass of flailing arms, spinning whistles and swaying trouser legs.

A wash of warped images with sounds asynchronous to their source, the film feels ghostly and unreal.

The idea that people came, and continue to come, together like this seems strange – impossible even. Leckey's film – made a half-decade after the 1994 Criminal Justice Bill – laments a lost time, but losses since are larger. The post-millennium music narrative is one of commercialisation, corporatisation, hostile legislation, club closures and persecution.

Within the film are flashes of utopia, but it takes attention to see them. Beyond the twisted limbs, wide eyes, locked jaws and loose tongues lies something greater. Mike Skinner, aka The Streets, said in his track 'Weak Become Heroes ': "They could settle wars with this. If only they will / Imagine the world's leaders on pills." The last shot of *Fiorucci Made Me Hardcore* is the same serene one it starts with. A man atop a tower, standing against that same oceanic blue. The sunset breaks and night becomes day again. 5am, friends and good music. Nothing could be better, surely anyone can see that ◎

Matt is a freelance writer and programmer.

Directed by Stanley Tucci, Campbell Scott, 1996
Words by Beth Webb,
Illustration by Allison Filice, Type by Simon Hayes

BIG Night

This charming, mid-'90s American indie is one of the all-time great foodie films.

The humbling, unifying effects of a good meal can be pinned to one particular scene in Stanley Tucci and Campbell Scott's 1996 feature, *Big Night*; a mouth-watering crescendo where brothers Primo and Secondo (Tucci and Tony Shalhoub) lift a dull metal drum to reveal a golden, richly soaked timpano – a giant, pasta-based pie.

The way they pat its sides and listen closely to hear the density of the meat and handmade pasta, hugged tightly by a warm shell before they serve it up to friends and neighbours feels almost parental, like they're nurturing this delicious product of their heritage and their craft.

"To eat good food is to be close to God," says Ian Holm's wealthy restaurateur, and you don't half notice it as patrons cast their eyes to the heavens, quietly and unanimously stunned by the bounty in front of them. *Big Night* isn't an especially well-made film – there are some editing flourishes that are better left in the '90s and the direction sometimes feels a little clunky. Yet it captures an undeniable spirit, not just in the food but in the message of giving something your all, even if there's a strong chance you'll fail ◉

Beth is a film journalist and programmer for the Bechdel Test Fest.

Directed by Krzysztof Kieslowski, 1991
Words by Justine Smith,
Illustration by Allison Filice, Type by Simon Hayes

The Double Life of Veronique

Two identical strangers find their lives intersecting.

In Krzysztof Kieslowski's metaphysical *The Double Life of Veronique*, two young women share the same face and the same soul. These two Veronicas, one living in Paris and the other in Poland, are separated by the imagined boundaries of politics. The politics of Kieslowski's cinema lies in the implicit. Thus, at first glance, the film only vaguely exists in our modern world. Politics are often interpreted in the grand gestures of obstruction and liberation, yet most of our lives muddle on regardless of who holds power. Weronika in particular, who lives in Poland as a singer, seems passively limited by living under communist rule.

In one crucial moment, there is a hint that the two women almost meet in Krakow Square during a protest. Weronika drops her sheet music and when she glances up, she sees her doppelganger taking photos and climbing onto a tourist bus. It is only much later when Veronique sees the photos of her trip that she takes notice of her look-alike – but it's too late. Weronika is dead.

Structuring this meeting around a moment of liberation and the impending collapse of the Soviet Union hints at the layers of limitations on the human spirit in a divided world. Kieslowski's films deal with the accidental meetings of fate and the improbability of love in a world that often seems cold and cruel. In *The Double Life of Veronique*, two women destined for each other never have the chance to meet due to the invisible constraints of politics. Even the transcendent power of art and love are limited within the film, contained by imagined boundaries. Kieslowski creates a film of such self-evident beauty, that the film itself serves as a thesis for a united world concerned with the small joys of the human experience ◉

Justine is a freelance writer and caffeine lover.

Twilight's
LAST GLEAMING

**Directed by
Robert Aldrich**

1977

Words by
Glenn Heath Jr

Illustration by
Pepa Prieto Puy

Type by
Justin Poulter

*Burt Lancaster has the
codes to blow up Earth.
Will he put us out of our
collective misery?*

I t's the end of the world as we know it, and Donald Trump feels fine. After months of political jockeying and threats of nuclear war, his much-ballyhooed meeting with North Korean leader Kim Jong-un is set for tomorrow. First though, some prep work: cabinet members, policy makers, and congressional Republicans gather for movie night.

According to top advisors, tonight's selection, 1977's *Twilight's Last Gleaming* by Robert Aldrich, will help to galvanise the proverbial troops. Trump is skeptical, though. He doesn't watch old movies. And the runtime is 146 minutes. That's just too long. At least McDonald's have provided the catering.

The lights dim, and a grainy still of the Statue of Liberty inspires applause, as does the familiar tune that plays over the image – "My Country Tis of Thee" performed by Billy Preston. Good, Trump thinks, a film about America. Across the theatre, stalwart young staffers parrot their bosses clapping for patriotic iconography. But their exuberance doesn't last long.

Definitions of lunacy dictate how you interpret *Twilight's Last Gleaming*, a scathing indictment of national repression. Burt Lancaster's disgraced USAF general could be construed as crazy for threatening nuclear war with Russia in order to

reveal the true traumas of the Vietnam War, but even more so for thinking the shadowy American government would actually bend to his will.

Is it more insane to think that politicians could actually learn from past sins, or that one of them would actually sacrifice their own life (as Charles Durning's president does) in order to sustain our beloved democracy? What about the treacherous doctrine of presidential credibility referenced throughout? Are we as a country great enough to survive the truth?

These questions – and countless more – race through the minds of the young White House staffers as credits roll. Upon exiting the theatre their bosses remain indifferent, occasionally rumbling, "Good action, cool split screens, but totally implausible."

Trump agrees, but adds one question as everyone disperses: "So who was the villain?" See you all tomorrow, maybe ◎

Glenn is the film critic for San Diego CityBeat *and Managing Director of Pacific Arts Movement.*

Directed by Charlie Chaplin, 1940
Words by Pamela Hutchinson
Illustration by Roca Balboa, Type by Justin Poulter

In which a Jewish barber takes on his despot doppelganger.

Perhaps it's naïve to believe that the assembled world leaders and corporate chiefs would fully absorb Charlie Chaplin's sublime, heartfelt plea for peace, humanity, compassion and unity, but we can hope. The world of *The Great Dictator*, like ours, is riven by prejudice and hate, and the vindictiveness and rivalries of politicians are about to precipitate global war. Chaplin shows that horror from the ground up – from the terror and violence in the Jewish ghetto, to the tyrant Hynkel, leader of Tomainia, callously deciding the fate of citizens on a whim, behind a desk in his gilded palace.

The CEOs might take note that this is also a world in which great leaps forward in technology have been used for evil ends: for Chaplin it's the aeroplane and the radio, for us it would be the internet, which promised liberty and comes laced with surveillance and manipulation.

They should all be worried about the resilience of solidarity, as seen in the spectacle of the people rebelling against a diabolical regime. Paulette Goddard's fearless insurgent battles the stormtroopers while Commander Schultz collaborates with the resistance because of a friendship forged in another war, the lessons of which have still not been learned. If they can't get any of that into their thick and cosseted heads, I'd like them to at least gaze at Hynkel bouncing a featherlight globe around his ludicrous state rooms, or playing childish games involving barber's chairs and mountains of spaghetti with his counterpart from the nation of Bacteria. Then they'd learn from this film something that may really disturb them: that they're fools, and we're laughing at them ◎

Pamela is a freelance writer and critic. Or so she claims!

Directed by John Landis, 1983
Words by Caroline Golum, Illustration by Roca Balboa, Type by Justin Poulter

TRADING PLACE$

On the enforced life-swapping antics of Eddie Murphy and Dan Aykroyd.

As eminent author and satirist Mark Twain once quipped, "History doesn't repeat itself, but it does rhyme." To wit: with the US beset by disastrous drug crises, record income inequality, rampant culture wars, and a senile television personality installed at the White House, now is the perfect time to revisit John Landis' *Trading Places*; an ingenious, Reagan-era update of Mark Twain's 'The Prince and the Pauper'. Boasting career-making turns by Eddie Murphy and Dan Aykroyd – as an inept Philadelphia street hustler and a tight-fisted Brahmin, respectively – it coats tough medicine about the tired "nature-versus-nurture" debate with a ribald candy shell.

Although centred around the two stars and their life-altering swap on the economic ladder, veteran thespians Ralph Bellamy and Don Ameche – whose scheme to replace broker Aykroyd with Murphy's opportunistic panhandler – are the veritable lynchpin of the whole scenario. Like many of their ilk, the patrician robber barons' blatant disregard for human dignity and timeless devotion to Mammon is all one big laugh – until Prince and Pauper find solidarity in their shared plight and bring the nefarious pair to financial ruin. Precious little has changed, unfortunately, since the initial release of Landis' razor-sharp comedy, but the world's titans would do well to revisit the message here: a little brotherhood (and backdoor accounting) is all it takes to shake the cracked foundation of capitalism to its core ◎

Caroline is a filmmaker & writer living in Brooklyn.

SPRING, SUMMER, AUTUMN, WINTER... AND SPRING

Directed by **Kim Ki-duk**		Words by **Anton Bitel**	
	2003	Illustration by **Roca Balboa**	Type by **Justin Poulter**

The life of a Buddhist apprentice is charted in accordance with the changing seasons.

In the centre of a remote lake surrounded by mountains, there is a floating world: a temple that is also a microcosm, where, in chapters corresponding to the seasons in rotation, *Spring, Summer, Autumn, Winter... and Spring* tracks a boy going through the stages of life, under the eyes of his Master, of Buddha, and (naturally) of us. Along this cyclical journey, the apprentice commits various wrongs - acts of cruelty, lust, murder and sacrilege. Though conventionally punished, the apprentice must also drag the burden (both a literal millstone and a more metaphorical weight) of his misdeeds for the rest of his life, on the steep, slippery path to becoming a Master himself.

Kim Ki-duk's film is a parable of sin, suffering and of wisdom acquired through misstep. Its broad frame – Buddhist rather than Christian – has no room for redemption or forgiveness, but plenty for contemplation and gradual, hard-earned transformation. Kim invites us, like the mountain-top Buddha, to see a wider panorama wherein human transgressions, though neither overlooked nor excused, form part of a bigger picture. Accordingly this long, unflinching view of male errancy is nuanced, refusing either to rush to judgment or to reduce a man merely to his crimes.

Kim is expressly implicated in this picture by playing the film's apprentice himself, in his self-abasing adulthood – as though the filmmaker is caught up in the same life struggle as his unequivocally transgressive protagonist. Having recently been accused of onset bullying, abuse and even rape in real life, Kim now comes with, putting it mildly, heavy baggage of his own. As we watch this man trying to transcend his sins, that mountain lake's waters may now seem muddier - but watch we should, unwaveringly, with a critical distance that neither ostracises nor exonerates ◉

Anton lances free in a world of horror.

Directed by **Diego Echeverria**	Words by **Ian Mantgani**
1984	Illustration by **Pepa Prieto Puy**

Pre-hipster Brooklyn receives a fascinating appraisal from its residents.

The prime movers of government and industry are people who already sit through many urgent presentations and conjure endless utopian schemes, so if they were my cinema audience, I think I'd like to give them transport to a time and a place, rather than explicitly obvious advocacy. A piece of direct cinema like *Los Sures* is a rooted and observational capsule of a movie, and a profoundly thought-provoking one about how citizens struggle to make humanity and society work.

The documentary, funded by US public television and the National Endowment for the Arts, takes place in Williamsburg in the mid-1980s, when the now hipster mecca was the poorest neighbourhood in Brooklyn and predominantly occupied by Latinos. Among general street scenes are testimonies from Tito, who strips cars; Marta, a single mother of five; Ana Maria, an older lady who soothes life's pain with religious faith; Cuso, a construction contractor who notes that money to regenerate the neighbourhood often ends up employing people from elsewhere while his neighbours go jobless; and Evelyn, who works in a women's community group.

They're all people striving to support their families and community, which is marked by poverty and addiction but also creativity and a sense of identity. What one gets from *Los Sures*, hopefully, is not an impulse to draft regeneration plans but a sense that the world is full of individuals capable of self-determination, and caution against flyover governance. The film has a material legacy beyond its 58-minute running time, too: its restoration in 2014, and a subsequent people's history documentary project, has energised community reflection on the evolution of Williamsburg, and is an object lesson in the power of film to validate the memory of a way of life, as well as the importance of public funding of the arts ◉

Ian is a filmmaker, writer and programmer based in London who has also worked on numerous US political campaigns.

I LIVE IN FEAR

The Japanese maestro takes on nuclear anxiety.

I would want our world leaders to be reminded of the fact that, while they take turns to play god, showcasing their weapons of mass destruction, humanity continues to suffer and we as individuals are left being ruled by fear. Toshiro Mifune gives a heartbreaking performance as a man so terrified by what he believes to be the imminent threat of nuclear war, that it ultimately destroys him. This feels especially relevant now during an increasingly tense nuclear stand off, and I hope the powerful and the super rich would open their eyes and see that their relentless pursuit of money and power can have a devastating effect on our everyday lives. The perpetual threat of catastrophic harm to human life can be as damaging to the mind as the reality can be to the physical body. Life is much too precious to be wasting it on fear

Tuppence Middleton is a British actor most recently seen in the Wachowskis' Netflix series, Sense8.

Directed by Akira Kurosawa, 1955
Words by Tuppence Middleton, Type by Simon Hayes

Follow the yellow brick road...

The Wizard of Oz, every time. That intoxicating mix of jeopardy, childlike wonderment, high camp and nostalgia couldn't fail to humble the most hardened of hearts. And is there another moment in cinema that comes as close to summing up the miracle of projected film as powerfully as the moment when black-and-white turns to colour?

Penny is the editor-in-chief of The Gentlewoman.

Directed by Victor Fleming, 1939
Words by Penny Martin, Type by Simon Hayes

A harrowing, docu-realistic rendering of the Algerian War.

No other political film in the last 50 years bears the same power to move you – and few remain as painfully relevant so many years later. A pinnacle of provocative cinema made strategically for social change. Director Gillo Pontecorvo radically redefines film's capacity to speak to current events. Pontecorvo, along with actors Ali La Pointe (Brahim Haggiag), Colonel Mathieu (Jean Martin), El-hadi Djafar (Saadi Yacef), and composer Ennio Morricone, work together to create a dynamic, gripping tapestry that immediately puts me in 1950s Algiers. Watching it now, it still lays bare the many struggles writhing throughout the world today

Efe Çakarel is the founder and CEO of MUBI.

Directed by Gillo Pontecorvo, 1966
Words by Efe Çakarel, Type by Simon Hayes

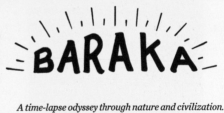

A time-lapse odyssey through nature and civilization.

This film is both powerful and moving and is as vast and grand as it is intimate and poetic. Explore the world, explore other cultures, explore humanity, explore yourself. Just explore.

Jarod is a Senior Film Programmer for SXSW.

Directed by Ron Fricke, 1992
Words by Jarod Neece, Type by Simon Hayes

HELP!

Directed by Richard Lester, 1965, Words by Abbey Bender, Illustration by Filippo Fontana, Type by Justin Poulter

John, Paul, George and Ringo are up to mischief.

There's no mood lifter quite so potent as a Beatles movie. *Help!* is undeniably silly, finding the fab four embroiled in a slapstick plot that features ample opportunities for pop spectacle. The powerful decision-makers of the world, foul as many of them may be, should be forced to watch something fun, something pure – I don't want to use cinema as a punishment. In moments of ennui, I often find myself thinking of The Beatles palling about in their colourful, ultra-'60s shared home, or frolicking through the snow together. *Help!* is filled with iconic proto-music videos of, essentially, The Beatles doing random fun stuff. I distrust anyone who doesn't want to watch that. While I know this hypothetical screening wouldn't necessarily bring about world peace, I do think it would lighten the mood, injecting some much-needed colour and humour into a bleak setting, and everybody likes the songs. For an hour and a half, I want to provide escapism, and *Help!* offers all kinds of escape – escape into nostalgia, escape to exotic locales, escape to a cinematic world where logic doesn't really matter – and in 2018 all these modes of escape sound pretty darn good ◎

Abbey is a New York-based writer on film and fashion.

Directed by Conan Le Claire, 1978 Words by Charles Bramesco, Illustration by Filippo Fontana, Type by Justin Poulter

FACES OF DEATH

An, err, informative examination of mortality in unflinching close up.

Roger Ebert said the movies are a machine to generate empathy, but I can't imagine the dim, brutish people leading in state or industry being moved by the sort of art I find moving. (I'm partial to the colossally ambitious, life-affirming stuff, your *Magnolias*, your *Dekalogs*, what-have-you). This hypothetical exercise sounds like it would devastate me with a reminder that most people who run the country operate on a different emotional frequency than I do.

My only recourse would be to go cynical, and to go hard. In *Tropic Thunder*, Tom Cruise's character says that actors aren't adults and accordingly can't be reasoned with on a grown-up's level, that all a person can do is pull their pants down and spank their arse. I believe a similar principle applies here – that the only way to get through to the likes of Trump, Zuckerberg, and Bezos would be through force rather than appealing to some base measure of humanity. So, once everyone's gotten nice and settled in their seats, spidery metal rods would burst out from the headrest and forcibly hook the audience's eyes open, Ludovico-style, at which point I'd begin screening *Faces of Death*. Force them all to overdose on suffering, and then maybe they'll reflexively double over in displeasure next time they approve a drone bombing or glance past factory mortality rates. To replace the child metaphor with one even more cynical: you can't teach a dog to understand why ripping up the couch is wrong, but you sure can punish him until he stops ◎

Charles is a freelance critic living in Brooklyn, and enjoys a good dolly shot.

ETERNAL SUNSHINE OF THE SPOTLESS MIND

	Directed by **Michel Gondry**	Words by **Emma Fraser**
	2004	Illustration by **Filippo Fontana** · Type by **Justin Poulter**

Jim Carrey and Kate Winslet can't forgive – so they try to forget.

Mary (Kirsten Dunst) in *Eternal Sunshine of the Spotless Mind* is armed with the perfect quotes to impress her crush. The crush that has already been consummated, erased from her memory and experienced once again. Quotes can be wielded in a number of ways – see Pinterest boards, Etsy and Instagram for ideas to frame, embroider or speak aloud – and they can be shaped to fit any narrative. For Mary she uses the words of Friedrich Nietzsche and Alexander Pope to reinforce the notion that erasing painful memories is a blessing, to be in the dark is illuminating. She uses these quotes as a way to impress, stumbling on the name "Pope Alexander" because she is nervous and stoned. A highly relatable flirting technique gone array. At the turn of the 20th century, Spanish philosopher George Santayana wrote, "Those who cannot remember the past are condemned to repeat it", and variations of this line have been uttered to underscore how little world leaders have paid attention to what came before. Instead of learning from history, it has been ignored and forgotten. Sometimes it feels like vast swathes of powerful people have undergone an erasure procedure. Instead of an ex, it's memories of events that have led to this point. In a world where "alternative facts" have become a catch-all for an excuse to lie, where Russian bots are the Lacuna, Inc. of the internet; erasing an ex in retaliation is a tit-for-tat lesson in how you can end up regretting something when you are too far gone to stop it. Joel (Jim Carrey) wants to call it off, but can't. Love is messy and painful – being in charge of a nuclear arsenal has more far-reaching and terrifying consequences. And the only Agent Orange you have to worry about in *Eternal Sunshine* is the colour of Kate Winslet's hair ◉

Emma is a freelance writer and wishes she had the bag packing skills of Grace Kelly in Rear Window.

AMERICAN MARY

	Directed by **The Soska Sisters**	**Words by** Katherine McLaughlin
	2012	**Illustration by** Roca Balboa / **Type by** Laurène Boglio

An eager medical student discovers an unconventional way to practice her craft.

Highlighted by recent events in the film industry, but a constant concern for women in any field, is the way we are set up to fail in the workplace due to our gender. When *American Mary* was released in the UK back in 2013 I made a knowing comment on Twitter asking, "Where are all the reviews written by women?" At the time of the film's release, I checked Rotten Tomatoes and couldn't find any. Checking now, out of 48 reviews, there are still only six penned by female writers.

The tweet was meant as playful provocation and it felt great to be able to voice a nagging frustration so early on in my career. This wasn't an outrageous feminist statement, but by simply pointing out a fact, I lost a number of followers. Perhaps people who didn't want to hear about the disproportionately small number of female directors regularly working compared to men, or the maddening gender imbalance within film criticism, were the ones who unfollowed. Who knows?

With a captive audience of world leaders and heads of industry, I would show a film about how young women can be driven to desperation and to compromise their morals by an unfair system. With *American Mary*, the Soska Sisters deliver a confrontational feminist body horror exploring how atrociously women are treated as they strive to achieve their dream careers.

My first time watching the film, I was truly in awe of their fearless criticism of the male gaze and its harmful effects on the psyche. Its gory trappings were inspired by personal experience and were used as a way for the twin directors to out monstrous men they'd dealt with in the film industry. The Soska sisters didn't pay heed to notes on their script to "make sure tits come out" in a rape scene – by ignoring those in charge they crafted a truly uncompromised vision ◎

Kat is a freelance writer who specialises in horror.

Directed by Guy Maddin, 2000
Words by Phil Concannon,
Illustration by Roca Balboa, Type by Laurène Boglio

THE *Heart* OF THE *World*

A film that is – quite literally – about movies saving the world.

When the fate of the world hangs in the balance, we don't have time for epics. Directed with the propulsive energy of silent-era Soviet propaganda, Guy Maddin's *The Heart of the World* presents a love triangle that's set against a backdrop of impending destruction. For brothers Osip and Nikolai, the only thing on the agenda in their final 24 hours is to vie for love of Anna, the state scientist who has announced the apocalypse.

While the two lovelorn young men compete to impress the object of their affections, and the rest of the citizens collapse into panic or indulge in drunken orgies, Anna sees the bigger picture, venturing to the core herself to save mankind. In the space of six frenzied, invigorating minutes, Maddin has drafted an apocalyptic scenario, diagnosed the root of our ills (it's no coincidence that the world's fatal heart attack is triggered when Anna is seduced by a fat capitalist), and offered an inspiring solution. The men, consumed by their own petty squabbles, eventually recede into the background allowing a heroine to take centre stage and become, in the film's words, "The new and better heart!" and how is this salvation celebrated? Through the immortal magic of projected images – "Kino! Kino! Kino!" *The Heart of the World* tells us that woman is the future of man, and cinema may yet save us all

Phil is a freelance writer and programmer trying to save the world one 35mm print at a time.

The Spider

A policeman and two criminals find themselves involved in a bizarre love triangle.

Directed by Robert Hamer, 1949
Words by Jaime Christley, Type by Laurène Boglio

When the highest-stationed people in the land know only to bash and gouge at enormous problems with heavy, stupid hands, characters who bear the weight of the world with an unwavering clarity as to the absurdity of it all must be our heroes. Robert Hamer's 1949 film has two such people: detective Maubert (Eric Portman) and criminal Lodocq (Guy Rolfe). Lodocq is a gentleman thief not by pretense but by actuality – raised on old money, he despises his ancestry and prefers to live only on money extracted from impregnable bank vaults. Maubert knows he's guilty of a string of robberies but can't sort out how, or why.

This premise, plus the girl (played by Romanian actress Nadia Gray) both men compete for, makes for a deceptively common, cozy policier that's unique in its balance between conveying the sheer magnitude of each man's compulsion, and their steadfast refusal to appear ruffled. The collision between unstoppable force and immovable object produces a winding itinerary that leads to an unexpected resolution, proving that none of the principals can withstand the tidal forces of a world cracked in half

Jaime is a film critic living in New York City.

The girl Chewing Gum

How better to inspire epiphany in an audience assured in its worldview(s) than screening a film that offers continual revelations and constantly challenges preconceptions? For me, that film is John Smith's monochrome avant-garde short, *The Girl Chewing Gum*.

The film opens with a shot of a busy intersection in Dalston, over which a traditionally omniscient voice-of-God narration (from Smith himself) directs the action seen on screen; "…and I want the little girl to run across…now." The world as prescribed by its creator/controller. What quickly becomes apparent, however, is that the voice is not directing the scene at all. The visual is documentary observation of the junction in East London, the soundtrack descriptions are an intentional assertion of authorial control on a disorderly reality.

As the unbroken shot continues for the length of a single reel of film, the voiceover becomes increasingly fantastical in its demands and detail.

The voice commands both space and time to move on its whim, seeing things invisible to the camera's eye and gleaning information about people's internal lives. The film may primarily lampoon cinematic conventions – the ego of the auteur, the 'reality' of documentary imagery – but it readily applies to similar social, cultural and political norms of the modern world

The Girl Chewing Gum can be plugged directly into contemporary concerns about the wielding of power, fake news, exploitable audiences and constructed narratives designed to cement a sense of dominion, or to lubricate acquiescence or unthinking consumption. That Smith achieves this in a remarkably funny and enjoyable 11 minutes makes it a perfect inoculation against a number of maladies afflicting today's industrial and political leaders

Ben is a freelance writer and programmer.

A witty undermining of cinema's inherent illusionism.

Directed by **John Smith**	Words by **Ben Nicholson**	Type by **Laurène Boglio**
1976	Illustration by **Diego Cadena Bejarano**	

QT's revisionist take on the final days of World War Two.

I would screen *Inglourious Bastards*, so that when it gets to the scene where the captive cinema audience gets burned to death, it would make them panic that it's all been an elaborate trick to do the same to them. When they leave the theatre still alive they might have a new appreciation for the precarious nature of their mortality, and from then on pull their heads out of their arses and start improving things ◉

Michael Sheen is a screen actor and activist.

Directed by Quentin Tarantino
Words by Michael Sheen, Type by Laurène Boglio

2009

A shafted veteran news anchor gets mad, but not necessarily even.

There are so many films! I'd screen Sidney Lumet's *Network*. It's just so timely now.

Babak Anvari is the director of Under the Shadow *and is currently filming a yet-to-be titled project.*

Directed by Sidney Lumet
Words by Babak Anvari, Type by Laurène Boglio

1976

1988

Directed by Isao Takahata
Words by Guillermo Del Toro,
Type by Laurène Boglio

One of the all-time great war movies care of Studio Ghibli.

I would screen *Grave of the Fireflies* to show that the greatest casualty of war is always innocence. The film's empathy and delicate balance of brutality and tenderness would strike deep. The enormous empathy and its ultimate belief in the possibility of love in the face of horror – these are things to be remembered now.

Guillermo dell Toro is a maker of flms and winner of awards.

13 LAKES

Directed by James Benning

2004

Words by
Mark Asch

Ilustration by
Roca Balboa

*A film about lakes.
Thirteen of 'em.*

In 1997, *New Yorker* correspondent Mark Singer rode on Donald Trump's private plane, where the gold leaf-encrusted developer manqué set out to watch the 1996 John Travolta vehicle *Michael*. "But [after] 20 minutes," Singer reported, Trump "got bored and switched to an old favorite [...] *Bloodsport*, which he pronounced 'An incredible, fantastic movie'." One of his adolescent sons was stationed by the VCR to fast-forward through everything but the parts where Jean Claude Van Damme is kicking somebody in the balls.

In so many ways, the Free World has precisely the leader it deserves. Trump, with his toilet-drinking dog's attention span, is merely the grossest articulation of a modern way of life flinching with a furious, fearful, crass, dazed distraction we never asked for, yet choose over and over again. When was the last time anyone was left alone with their own thoughts?

Every movie dictates to its viewer an experience of time. In *13 Lakes*, the most accurately titled film since the days of the *actualité*, experimental filmmaker James Benning offers up vistas of 13 American lakes, from the Alaskan peninsula to the Florida Everglades, the Grand Tetons to the headwaters of the Kennebec. The fixed frame is at once an abstract canvas, with bands of land and sky stacked above a rectangle of blue or gray water, and a landscape painting come alive with the sound of rushing water and birdsong, and the sight of boats, windblown clouds, or whatever crosses our field of vision during the ten minutes we spend in contemplation of each lake.

The film is a reminder of the beauty of our natural heritage and our responsibility to an Earth we continue to skullfuck, of course. But it's also a reverie in the tradition of American Transcendentalism, with its conception of the outdoors as a route inwards to the mind, and onwards to grace ◎

Mark is the Film Editor of Brooklyn Magazine *and a contributor to* Little White Lies, Film Comment, Reverse Shot *and elsewhere.*

THE BLUES BROTHERS

Directed by John Landis, 1980
Words by Edith Bowman, Illustrationa & Type by Laurène Boglio

Dan Akyroyd and John Belushi star in the original band reunion movie.

I think with the state of the world right now, everybody could do with some complete entertainment along with Carrie Fisher and probably one of the best car chases in cinematic history, all that and a good sing-along to all the amazing tunes. Nothing like singing and laughing to soothe and heal the soul. Comedy can be the best way to deal with distressing and difficult situations and subjects, so sit them down with Jake and Elwood and the brilliance of John Landis to solve all world problems.

Edith is a broadcaster and host of the very great film/music podcast, Soundtracking.

LOVELEss

Directed by Andrey Zvyagintsev, 2017
Words by Carol Salter, Type by Laurène Boglio

A bleak portrait of familial fracture direct from snowy Russia.

As the title suggests, we are part of an increasingly uncompassionate society lead by governments who are removed and detached. Andrey Zvyagintsev's haunting film *Loveless* is, for me, more than just a portrait of two parents' lack of love for their unwanted child as they fight bitterly through a divorce, I see this film as an allegory of where we are heading – lacking compassion and kindness as we move into a self-interested society. Don't let our world become a morally detached society without empathy. More love please!

Carol is the director of Almost Heaven.

AMBIANCé

Directed by Anders Weberg, 2020
Words by Timothy George Kelly, Type by Laurène Boglio

The longest film ever made that doesn't actually exist.

Ambiance is a 720-hour Swedish art film that I have absolutely no interest in seeing. I would like to lock all the police, political and business leaders in the world in a cinema with no food or water and make them watch this. As there is nothing more inspiring than a deadline, the 30 days to watch the film would be plenty of time for us plebs to redistribute all wealth, de-escalate climate change, destroy all military weapons, automate shit jobs, and still have lots of spare time to spend chilling and flirting with each other. This is a situation in which I can see movies possibly saving the world.

Timothy is the director of the documentary Brexitannia.

BFI LONDON
FILM FESTIVAL 2017
OFFICIAL SELECTION

WINNER
BEST MUSIC GHENT
FILM FESTIVAL

QUINZAINE
DES RÉALISATEURS
CANNES 2017

WINNER
EUROPA CINEMAS
LABEL AWARD 2017

WINNER
BEST DIRECTOR & BEST EDITOR
DAVID DI DONATELLO AWARD

"A FILM OF FEROCIOUS ENERGY AND OBSERVATIONAL KEENNESS"
JONATHAN ROMNEY, FILM COMMENT

VULTUREHOUND

"GRIPPING AND AUTHENTIC"
NEW INTERNATIONALIST

NEW INTERNATIONALIST

MARTIN SCORSESE PRESENTS   A FILM BY **JONAS CARPIGNANO**

THE CIAMBRA

OUR TERRITORY
IN CINEMAS JUNE 15

   LUXBOX

WWW.THECIAMBRA-FILM.COM   #OURTERRITORY   ☏ ✦ ✉ @peccapics

TEXAS *Chili*

1. TOMATO SAUCE

HARD SHELL PEPPERCORN

CHILLIES

HUMAN FLESH

The south will never rise again.

1986

Directed by
Tobe Hooper

| Words by David Jenkins | Type by Laurène Boglio |

Illustration by
Diego Cadena Bejarano

There's a moment in Tobe Hooper's *The Texas Chainsaw Massacre 2* where an old man has a chainsaw forcibly inserted into his rectum – but that's not why I've chosen to screen this film. If depictions in the modern media are anything to go by, it's the story of a very average southern family who happen to be cannibals. They find solace and shelter under a Confederate flag whose very fibres are held together with blood. As drunken yahoos charge around Texas unloading their six-shooters into the landscape, the Sawyer clan are co-opting the spirit of their fallen southern brethren and cultivating a sense of downhome pride with the help of industrial power tools, and they make a tidy profit in the process with all the prime meat they collect along the way.

Bill Moseley as Chop Top wears a Sonny Bono wig to cover the metal plate which keeps his brain from emptying out of his skull, a wound he incurred in Vietnam. The Sawyers are the product of isolationism and nationalism, and their nihilistic creed (which masquerades as patriotism) can be seen in their home: a disused theme park named Texas Battle Land (in actual fact the defunct Prairie Dell Lake Amusement Park whose fibreglass husk sits 50 klicks north of Austin). They are co-opting the spirit of the fallen South and maligning it for their own evil ends. Hooper's film offers an alarming exploration into a divided America, and screening this is the only way the nabobs up top will realise what the hell is going on ◉

David Jenkins is the editor of Little White Lies.

THE TEXAS CHAINSAW MASSACRE 2

Directed by
Miguel Arteta, 2017
Words by Brodie Lancaster,
Illustration by Diego
Cadena Bejarano,
Type by Laurène Boglio

The awkward dinner party is the subject of this comedy of abject embarrassment.

Writer Mike White's decade-long reckoning with what we owe to the world and each other began with *Year of the Dog* in 2007, continued with HBO's *Enlightened*, and reached its peak in the sharp and brutally empathetic *Beatriz at Dinner*.

The film is timely in its portrayal of a real estate tycoon who poaches animals for sport and assumes any brown person at a dinner party is there to serve him. But to frame a film like this and a character like Beatriz (Salma Hayek) only in the context of a Trump-y, Brexit-y world would be turning a blind eye to White's dedication to painting delicate tree-huggers as heroes.

Beatriz at Dinner captures the feeling of struggling to find peace between the clashing ideologies of confronting idealists. And it ultimately forces us to listen to people who are silenced or ignored in a way we wouldn't until they sit down at a table across from us and make us squirm a little ◎

Brodie is a pop culture critic who wrote this at a Harry Styles concert.

Directed by no-one, NEVER
Words by Lenny Abrahamson, Illustration
by Diego Cadena Bejarano, Type by Laurène Boglio

The director of Room *is sceptical that movies have the ability to change minds.*

I'd like to help, but... the assumption underlying your thought experiment is that these people just need to be touched by the right art in order to be transformed, to have their eyes opened. But their eyes are open! And I'm sure many have shed tears listening to beautiful music or been profoundly moved by great cinema without it making the slightest difference to how they operate politically. All good art is compassionate, but there's a limit to what it can do unless in sync with bigger forces. Of course I know I'm not supposed to take your request literally and that I'm a humourless git who's entirely missing the point, but, given the general grimness of the news at the moment, I just can't bring myself to join in the fun. If someone put a gun to my head, maybe I'd pick the longest film I could think of – at least it would keep them off the streets ◎

Lenny Abrahamson is the director of Room.

After Life

	Directed by Hirokazu Kore-eda	Words by Michael Leader	Type by Simon Hayes
	1998	Illustration by Diego Cadena Bejarano	

A philosophical Japanese gem which frames death as a blissful release.

I believe that the world could benefit from a bit of existential self-scrutiny, and few films have inspired a more desperate reassessment of my life to date than Hirokazu Kore-eda's 1998 fantasy-drama *After Life*. Kore-eda is now primarily known for his cosy, yet profound domestic dramas – *Still Walking*, *Our Little Sister*, *I Wish*, et al – but *After Life* acts as the fulcrum for the director's whole career, sitting squarely between his early documentaries and festival-favourite fiction features.

It's Monday, and a group of people are welcomed into a rundown administrative building. They're all recently deceased, and must choose one memory from their lives to take with them into the hereafter, which will be recreated, captured on film and projected to the whole group at the end of the week. Across a series of interviews, the guests (some played by non-actors) discuss their lives with their assigned counsellors. Some hit upon their choices immediately, while others find it harder, paralysed by the very act of looking back over the years.

Meditating on memories is a rare luxury in our media-saturated modern world. It can be hard to find yourself among the tangle of personas, platforms and profiles that we navigate on a daily basis. The conversations inspired by *After Life*'s gently heightened metaphor could lead to significant, identity-unravelling realisations. As a film, it's a masterpiece, but as a blueprint for real-world activity – imagine worldwide workshops driven by compassion and communication, fuelled by cinema as an empathy engine – it could be the start of something bigger. All by posing what is, on the face of it, a very simple question: what memory would you choose? ◎

Michael is a freelance film critic, Editorial Director for Film4 Online *and co-founder of the Misc. Films programming collective.*

TEN

Directed by Abbas Kiarostami, 2002
Words by Stephen Cone, Type by Simon Hayes

A lilting portrait of modern Tehran as seen through the eyes of a female motorist.

An experimental masterpiece not-so-hidden behind a reality TV veneer, what more vital mortar-shot of a film to place within the view of world leaders than this heartbreaking 21st century expression of human rights, progress, liberation, repression, sadness and struggle. The melancholic strains of Howard Blake's music for the British television classic *The Snowman*(!) accompany the most complex and moving fade to black in movies, bringing it home.

Stephen is the director of the excellent film Princess Cyd *which you should see.*

A Field in England

Directed by Ben Wheatley, 2013
Words by Michael Smiley, Type by Simon Hayes

Mad existential larks abound in this no-fi dirty bomb of pastoral psychedelia.

"Thanks to you we're all fucked, just some of us get to wear a big hat!"

Michael is a screen actor who hails from Belfast Ireland.

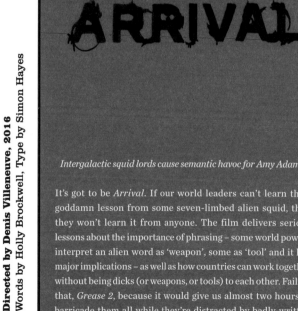

Directed by Florian Henckel von Donnersmarck, 2006
Words by Colin Trevorrow, Type by Simon Hayes

A German Stasi agent questions his dedication to the socialist cause.

Empathy and compassion are common ingredients in social and political change. Listening to a perceived enemy is a first step toward understanding. This film is a beautiful reminder of that.

Colin Trevorrow lives on a farm and is the director of Safety Not Guaranteed, Jurassic World *and* The Book of Henry.

Directed by Denis Villeneuve, 2016
Words by Holly Brockwell, Type by Simon Hayes

Intergalactic squid lords cause semantic havoc for Amy Adams.

It's got to be *Arrival*. If our world leaders can't learn their goddamn lesson from some seven-limbed alien squid, then they won't learn it from anyone. The film delivers serious lessons about the importance of phrasing – some world powers interpret an alien word as 'weapon', some as 'tool' and it has major implications – as well as how countries can work together without being dicks (or weapons, or tools) to each other. Failing that, *Grease 2*, because it would give us almost two hours to barricade them all while they're distracted by badly-written ensemble numbers.

Holly is a freelance tech writer and editor of Gadgette.com

	Directed by **Jonathan Demme**	Words by Josh Slater-Williams
	1984	Illustration and type by Laurène Boglio

David Byrne's suit gets progressively larger in this spectacular concert film.

A film by Jonathan Demme and Talking Heads, *Stop Making Sense* is not just a concert documentary. The case can be made that it's actually a musical given how it's put together. But it's not just a musical either. Watching it is akin to a religious experience. If heaven is a place, I imagine it to be like *Stop Making Sense*. It is magical. It is alive. It has a soul.

Given the opportunity, this is the one film I would show to world leaders and decision makers – suits with a say watching a guy in a big suit sway. I would look to see how far into it they can get without being emotionally overwhelmed; without achieving a euphoric state. I'd bet on about 20-ish minutes in, before 'Burning Down the House' wraps up, as a minimum for most.

I don't know what they'd expect staring at the cinema screen. But I'd hope they'd see it as a representation of what the world could be. It presents a spectacular, infectious vision of community and humanity. It shows what happens if we loosen up and allow the passion of others to dismantle the walls we put up around ourselves. Let them see there's a million ways to get things done. There's a million ways to make things work out.

Additionally, this is also the film I would screen for alien visitors from other planets who can't speak any of our languages. For hopefully peaceful extraterrestrials looking to share their knowledge with another world, I am optimistic that this exuberant 88-minute taste of mankind's potential would convince them this must be the place ◎

Josh is a freelance film and culture writer the BFI,
Sight & Sound and The Skinny, among others.

	Directed by **Alfred Hitchcock**	**Words by** James Luxford
	1948	**Illustration and type by** Laurène Boglio

A pair of ultra-smug students attempt to execute the perfect crime.

I n an era of fake news, ugly politics and false advertising, there's no better time to revisit Alfred Hitchcock's examination of the devastating consequences of ideas that expand to ideology.

The film is set during a dinner party in which the two hosts (John Dall and Farley Granger) have killed a former schoolmate and hidden him in a trunk that becomes the party's centrepiece. The motivation for the killing is a demonstration of superiority – to prove that their refined intellect could make murder an art form. Their plot is agonisingly unravelled over 80 minutes by their old schoolmaster, Rupert Cadell (James Stewart).

Stewart serves both as investigator and unwitting instigator in this murder mystery. A radical thinker, he casually espouses murder as a way of thinning out the inconveniences of society. "Think of the problems it would solve," he argues. "Unemployment, poverty, standing in line for theatre tickets". The party guests are shocked, but the true horror comes as Cadell learns that

his former students have taken his theoretical musings to a deadly end.

Released three years after World War Two, you can hear a ring of bitter experience from Stewart (an Air Force veteran) as he confronts the men: "By what right do you dare to say that there's a superior few to which you belong?" For Cadell, anguish mixes with guilt as he realises his rhetoric sowed the seeds that led to a man's murder. When clever words spoken to impress a crowd are taken literally, the innocent suffer. That is *Rope*'s message, perhaps as pertinent today as it was in the '40s. As information becomes increasingly easier to deliver or manipulate, I would hope my assembled audience would take this message on board ◎

James is a film journalist and broadcaster from London. He has written on film for The Guardian, The Hollywood Reporter, Metro, City AM *and the BBC.*

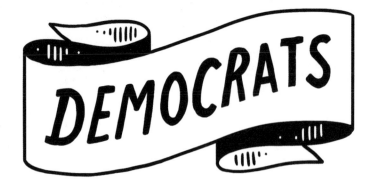

DEMOCRATS

Directed by Camilla Nielsson, 2014

Words by Guy Lodge
Illustration by Jason Ngai
Type by Laurène Boglio

My choice of film to show a group of gathered political leaders is, admittedly, a bit of a literal one: no lyrical metaphors or elegantly understated allegories for them. (After all, can you name many politicians with a flair for subtle poetic expression?) No, Camilla Nielsson's lucid, fascinating 2014 documentary is directly and dynamically about the hard graft of forging democracy. If "forging" seems a loaded choice of verb, all its meanings apply in this study of the tortuous negotiations that led to Zimbabwe's 2013 constitution, after Morgan Tsvangirai's Movement for Democratic Change forced a coalition government with Robert Mugabe's ruling ZANU-PF leadership in an ugly 2008 election. Curdled, compacted layers of corruption at the top are laid bare, as is the human difficulty of bringing about change even when you're holding some of the cards. Zimbabwe may be globally recognised as one of the world's most troubled, compromised democracies, yet many a leader from a more supposedly functional nation should recognise themselves in this pained, fragile process, and wince ◎

South African-born and London-based, Guy writes on film for Variety *and* The Observer.

Following the contentious Zimbabwe election in 2008, a coalition government works to rewrite the country's constitution.

Directed by Howard Hawks, 1962
Words by Matt Thrift,
Illustration and type by Jason Ngai

A jocular paean to friendship and the joys of being part of a gang.

I n the months following the release of James Cameron's *Avatar* back in 2009, there were widely publicised accounts of certain audience members wishing they could relocate to Pandora, the film's fictional planet. Not all of us, even those who would consider themselves fans, shared the sentiment, despite the admittedly strong selling-point of a solid wifi network. It does beg the question of which cinematic milieu we might choose to up sticks to in its place, though. I'd assume it wasn't just the location that had fanatics pining for Pandora, but more the social and cultural traditions of the planet's inhabitants that led to *Avatar* being singled out for impossible gap year daydreams.

With similar criteria in mind, my fantasy Thomas Cook package would take me into the world of Howard Hawks' 1962 adventure film, *Hatari!* Sure, the sunny Tanzanian plains of its setting appeal, but they remain reachable within the realms of possibility. It's the vibe engendered by the film's lack of narrative concerns – there are barely any stakes in its 157 minutes – that see me returning to it so often; my fondness for it as the ultimate hang-out movie. There's a moral consistency that runs through the filmography of Hawks, a worldview enacted through his characters and applied to the dynamics of the group.

As *Hatari!* strolls through its numerous episodes with little sense of urgency, said dynamics become the focus of our attention. It's most apparent in the film's piano scene, a regular occurrence in the Hawks back catalogue. A musical negotiation of the outsider's acceptance into the tightly-knit posse, the scene paves the way for redressed balances within the team, Hawks bringing all into the frame on equal terms. It's no masterpiece, or the director's best film, but it possesses a humanism at once gentle and piercing. *Hatari!* may not be the film to change the world, but a few weeks spent in its company may just help us look on it with kinder eyes ◎

Matthew writes about films and he does not wear pyjamas.

Directed by Gregory Jacobs, 2015
Words by Ella Donald
Illustration by Allison Filice

MAGIC mike XXL

Mike and his merry band of strippers embark on one last ride.

What can transcend all language, cultural, and social barriers to deliver joy? Please reserve all answers, for they are meaningless – Joe Manganiello grinding against a gas station soft drink fridge in the American South to the Backstreet Boys is the only one that makes sense. Anticipation for *Magic Mike XXL*, the sequel to Steven Soderbergh's 2012 male entertainer-focused drama that looked like a film ready for girls-night-out screenings but was actually about post-global financial crisis life, was initially shrug-worthy. But *XXL* is a Trojan of a different kind – one of the most glorious surprises of moviegoing in recent memory, that wasn't just made for a girls-night-out label, but indeed reinvented what that means and what it can do.

Audiences don't just walk out of *Magic Mike XXL*, they emerge having been enlightened by the likes of Jada Pinkett Smith's emcee and club owner, persuasive enough to successfully lead a cult in dubbing her patrons 'Queens'. It's a megaplex lesson about male vulnerability, masculinity, female pleasure and equality both in the bedroom and out, delivered with a female gaze and a confident slide into the next dance number or overt display of titillation.

It doesn't just play to but rather pamper the female audience, while challenging the men around them to do better, with little more than a loose-playing conversation in the back of a van driving across the American south, or a strategically placed needle drop. "We're like healers or something," crooner Andre (Donald Glover) says. Heal the world with *Magic Mike XXL* ◉

Ella is a journalist and university tutor from Australia. You can probably find her rewatching Halt and Catch Fire.

Directed by John Henry Timmis IV, 1987
Words by Adam Woodward, Illustration by Allison Filice

the CURE for INSOMNIA

5,220 minutes of unalloyed visual punishment.

Movies *can* save the world, but we all know that real change comes from the bottom up. It's naive to think that the key holders to our collective future could ever be steered in the same direction by a single galvanising viewing experience. There are simply too many vested interests undermining common sense decision-making these days, too many inflated egos blocking the path to progress. Besides, why waste a golden opportunity to troll those responsible for the sorry mess we're in? Call me cynical/petty/both, but in the name of good clean schadenfreude I would gladly track down a copy of John Henry Timmis IV's "lost" freeform epic from 1987 – an 87-hour exercise in endurance cinema consisting of the poet Lee Groban reciting his own dense prose, randomly interspersed with stock footage of hardcore pornography and heavy metal music. That'll teach 'em. Fuckers ◉

Adam is the digital editor of Little White Lies.

We live in PUBLIC

Directed by **Ondi Timoner**	Words by **Sophie Monks Kaufman**
2009	Illustration by **Allison Filice**

A profile of a dot-com millionaire with a penchant for social experiments.

Ondi Timoner began filming dot-com millionaire Josh Harris in 1999. He was famous in New York for his parties and dubbed "The Warhol of the Web". She went on to capture his social experiments. Despite the scuzzy, lo-fi visuals they speak with biting clarity to the virtual manner in which we live how.

An art project dubbed 'Quiet' ran as the new millennium loomed and saw participants living in a camera-covered bunker. "Everything is free except the video we capture of you. That we own," smirked Harris who remained discreetly away from the primal anarchy within his reality TV-style setup. Not so for his next trick. *We Live In Public* involved surveilling a loft he shared with girlfriend, Tanya Corrin. There were cameras in the bathroom, cameras in the bedroom and – most toxically – a chat window which enabled he and Tanya to see what viewers were saying about them. After a fight they would rush to their monitors to check who was said to have won.

Voluntary erosion of privacy is now the status quo online. Timoner is sympathetic in fleshing out the background of a man driven to commodify the personal. Her balanced perspective only strengthens the cautionary tale which emerges across 90 minutes (sculpted from 5000 hours and 10 years of footage). These truths were ever thus but are intensified by our constant freedom to put ourselves on display: posturing hollows out a person consumed with performing rather than embodying their humanity. Seeking more connections can lead to losing the ones which mean the most. At a time in human history when greed is good when it comes to the number of one's followers, *We Live In Public* serves as a reminder to count what you have in private ◉

Sophie is the contributing editor of Little White Lies *but otherwise defies categorisation.*

They Came Together

**Directed by
David Wain**

2014

**Words by
Manuela Lazic and Adam Nayman**

**Illustration by
Filippo Fontana**

**Type by
Justin Poulter**

A New York candy store stand-off which leads to... love?

"Do I find you cute and funny? Yes. Could you be the guy that I fall for and live with forever? Yes. But the point is you're a corporate robot. And so it is with great pleasure that I say to you, go jump in a lake, meathead!" After this tirade, Amy Poehler's Molly throws her glass (of water) at Paul Rudd's Joel, and storms out of the room. Molly and Joel came together to this costume party, and although they're both dressed like Founding Father Benjamin Franklin, the two Americas they represent couldn't be further apart.

David Wain's rigorously political 2014 film *They Came Together* presents us with an unlikely couple trying to bridge the divide between their hearts and minds — a meet-cute in the shadow of late capitalism. Molly's independent candy store, Upper Sweet Side, finds itself threatened by the encroachment of the monolithic Candy Systems and Research (CSR), the corporation that Joel works for. Seven decades after Lubitsch, the *Shop Around the Corner* is a high-rise.

Molly and Joel's dynamic represents a conflict all too common in our unsentimental age of gentrification and unregulated trade. Yet the extent to which Molly lives outside processes of exchange – her candy is free – is an impossible dream. The director's purpose, however, is not pure realism (as it is in *Wet Hot American Summer*). Rather, he appeals to our fantasist tendencies and dreams of a better world. *They Came Together* follows the tropes of the romantic comedy only to turn them inside out and reveal their basis – and power – in reverie and idealism.

It is typical of Wain's sociological savvy that Joel explicates the difference between communism and totalitarianism during coffee talk, while the seemingly socialist Molly barely apologises for her white supremacist parents (name a more prescient studio comedy in the 21st century). Ultimately, *They Came Together* is a parable about learning to see things from the other side: falling in love as understanding. Joel's transformation is most apparent: in an impassioned speech to the CSR board, he suggests that there's room for two candy stores in New York. Compromise is the dream come true.

Our hero finds a new way – his own coffee shop, called "Cup of Joel", modelled after Molly's modest mom-and-pop operation. Yet suddenly, reality bursts in and his and Molly's shops fail miserably, as well as the pair's relationship (a coda revealing their break-up surpasses the ripped-off ending of *La La Land*). But the very last lines imply that the fantasy survives. Not only does *They Came Together* suggest that give-and-take is a necessity in business and romance alike (a lesson with endless implications for a globalised society) but it believes in the importance of following your heart. Even if dreams of a better world are repeatedly crushed, they bring people together, time and again. Screening this masterpiece at the United Nations' headquarters in Manhattan would not only honour the film's setting, but its message; it's almost like idealism is another character in the movie ◉

Manuela is a freelance film critic from France and Adam Nayman is one of her best friends. Adam lives in Toronto and doesn't regret this essay.

Directed by Joel and Ethan Coen, 1996
Words by Hannah Woodhead
Illustration by Laurène Boglio

Woodchippers, eh?

It's a beautiful day.

The bright winter sun will eventually melt away the crimson-streaked snow up by Moose Lake. Marge Gunderson knows that. She knows that the world spins madly on, and men will always kill men for a little bit of money. "I just don't understand it," she glumly tells Gaear Grimsrud, who stares at her blankly from the back seat of her police cruiser.

There's so much that feels incomprehensible about the world in its current state. You can know the logical, technical reasons for global conflict, rising sea levels and the presence of a snarling tangerine megalomaniac as Leader of the Free World, but knowledge, as it turns out, isn't power. The inherent goodness of police chief Marge Gunderson is the warm ray of light which breaks the morning in *Fargo*, and she stands alone as a totem for hope in a cold, cold world. I've long-since concluded that humans are inherently not very nice to one another, and can offer no insight into whether this is nature or nurture. The world will burn up and burn back again, and all we can do is make the best of what we have. Try to be better.

"Heck Norm, y'know, we're doing pretty good," Marge says to her husband when he laments the fact his mallard painting didn't make it onto the first-class postage stamp. A simple reflection amid 98 minutes of bungled bloodshed. It's so easy to miss the poetry in Marge Gunderson's optimistic observation, and I'm not naive enough to think we can do anything to reverse thousands of years of misery built on misery. But if we're all going to die anyway, it might as well be to the tune of Carter Burwell's melodic score, while the sun rises on another beautiful Minnesotan morning ◎

Hannah is the social producer for Little White Lies.

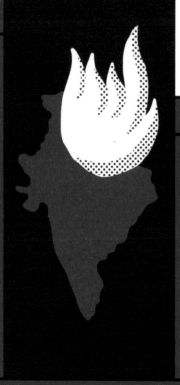

Directed by Mehboob Khan, 1957
Words by Christine Molloy and Joe Lawlor
Illustration by Laurène Boglio

MOTHER INDIA

A gaudy and glorious Bollywood classic which throws everything and more into the pot.

The film we would screen for this special audience is *Mother India* (1957) by Mehboob Khan. It was a family favourite of ours when our daughter was younger. It's a full on epic family drama, while also keeping ideas of a newly independent nation, moving on from the oppressions and humiliations of colonialism. Yes, it's long. Three hours long in fact. It has it all: slapstick comedy, great songs, sweeping storyline, archetypal characters (including a villainous moneylender), death in abundance, biblical floods, poverty beyond belief, and even filicide. The film puts you through the wringer and just when you think things can't get any worse, they do. It can be read in many complex ways, but we would want the attendant audience to focus on the themes of social inequality and the degradation and injustices of poverty. We would insist on no intervals or breaks for ice cream – we want this audience to be forced to endure. We wouldn't want them to get away lightly ◎

Christine and Joe make great movies and art. Their most recent work was 2016's Further Beyond

Come AND See

If you thought war was hell, you ain't seen nothing yet.

**Directed by
Elem Klimov, 1985
Words by
Christina Newland
Type by Laurène Boglio**

It's simply impossible to come away from *Come and See* unscathed. Portraying some of the Nazis' worst crimes during the Second World War, the film is both a lyrical and grotesque rumination on the experiences of one young boy (Aleksei Kravchenko) who joins the Belarusian army in the hopes of defending his charred, ransacked homeland. It might be the most convincing anti-war film ever made, purely through its uncompromising portrayal of human degradation. There are elements of horror in the very fabric of the film; a knotted dread at what fresh atrocity will soon appear.

Gather a group of eminent world leaders to see the transfixed, terrified face of young actor Kravchenko. He stares with vacant horror at an unseen – maybe nonexistent – object. His haunted, sunken eyes bulge from an almost supernaturally-aged face; he looks underfed, frog-like, with heavy lines in his brow. It seems impossible that this creature – so marked by trauma as to seem like a frightened animal – was once just a young boy. Five years ago, CNN reported on Syria's child refugees flooding into Lebanon with hair that had turned a trauma-induced grey. One infant was even born with a tuft of white hair. Still, the same horror befalls those children daily as the war rages on.

Klimov's genius is not merely in creating an onscreen victim of the war, but in breaking him down enough that an audience begins to feel estranged from that victimhood. His experiences effectively become an enormous gulf: in surpassing our worst nightmares, the distance between his humanity and our own grows curiously larger. Perhaps there's a slim chance that the people in charge might see his dehumanisation, his victimhood, and think again before beating their chests or turning their backs ◎

Christina Newland is a writer on film and culture with an appreciation for '70s American cinema and boxing flicks.

DANCE, GIRL, DANCE

**Directed by Dorothy Arzner, 1940
Words by Alicia Malone, Type by Laurène Boglio**

A proto-feminist masterpiece about an aspiring ballerina competing with a seasoned burlesque star.

Lately in Hollywood, there has been a lot of talk about women. This comes as a relief for me, someone who has always been vocal about the low number of women in powerful positions and how this affects not only the people working in film, but all of us who love film. Now, people are finally listening. The Time's Up and #MeToo movements have brought with them a wider conversation about the type of opportunities extended (or not extended) to women, and how female characters are treated on screen. I'm optimistic this conversation will lead to action, but Hollywood remains a boy's club.

If I had my way, I'd gather together some of the gatekeepers in the film industry and screen the 1940 film, *Dance, Girl, Dance*. It is directed by Dorothy Arzner, a woman whose story should be widely known in Hollywood but sadly isn't. Her achievements are inspiring – she was the only female director working in the studio system in the 1930s, and invented the boom microphone by putting a mic on the end of a fishing rod. She also made feminist films that were commercially successful, but *Dance, Girl, Dance* remained underground until the second-wave feminist movement in the 1970s. The film is a backstage musical, following a similar format to many studio films of the time, except with a distinctly female bent. It centres on two female dancers, played by Lucille Ball and Maureen O'Hara, who are pitted against one another and objectified in front of an audience of men. It's a fairly blistering satire about women being used for entertainment. Arzner asks the audience to examine their own objectification of the characters, showing how we too are complicit.

There's a scene right at the end, where Maureen O'Hara's character turns to the audience, frustrated at being yelled at to strip instead of dance her routine. She says, "I know you want me to tear my clothes off so you can look your 50 cents worth. 50 cents for the privilege of staring at a girl the way your wives won't let you. What do you suppose we think of you up here with your silly smirks your mothers would be ashamed of... What's it for? So you can go home when the show's over, strut before your wives and sweethearts and play at being the stronger sex for a minute?" It's quite a brutal speech, brilliantly directed and very forward-thinking for the time. So, because of this message, and because it shows a female filmmaker who should be known, one who was at the top of her game at a time when it was even harder for women. I would strap these studio heads down and make them watch *Dance, Girl, Dance*. And you know what? They'd probably enjoy it! ◎

Alicia is an LA-based writer and host for TCM, FlimStruck and Fandango

WATERSHIP DOWN

Directed by Martin Rosen, 1978
Words by Roxanne Sancto,
Illustration by Jason Ngai, Type by Laurène Boglio

Aboard, aboard Watership Down – a poem.

The invites are out,
the screens have been polished,
the seats are awaiting
the world's biggest asses.
Carrying clout over all to be demolished,
all to be killed, and how to operate us – the masses.
Tonight these seats shall constipate them,
until the aches shall explode
through piles of love and unity,
the viewing's harsh
but they'll comprehend, because, you see,
I slipped 'em some doves in their G&Ts.
The bunnies are out, my Schmidt front and centre,
aware of the impending apocalypse awaiting,
guests roll up and pout on the blood red carpets,
shameless eyes bright, oblivious to their fating.
Tonight these screens shall tune them in to
their own roles on Watership Down,
a theatre full of Hazel's descendants
cuddled by General Woundwort's
human equivalents.
Thank ye, ol' white dove.

The lights are out, the film plays on,
drinks bubble through clogged intestines,
the audience is peaking,
I can see their hearts sprout with love,
their guts pained with guilt,
their eyes are literally leaking.
Tonight, tonight nostalgic landscapes come to life
as I unleash my childhood trauma
on the predators we never saw coming.
One single film on a 24-hour loop
and at least ten bunnies doing a binkie – whoopee!
The lights go on, the come-down's nigh,
promises drown out all credits.
Drive on, drive on, in your barrels of sins,
be gone with your crocodile tears and hollow
words. I know your souls are sore.
Tonight, tonight sleep shall not find you
and you'll be haunted by my cuddly, floppy-
eared Schmidt.
And you know what?
You'll sweat and grind and scream his name
and he will not give a shit ◎

CRIMSON TIDE

Directed by Tony Scott, 1995
Words by Elena Lazic,
Illustration by Jason Ngai, Type by Laurène Boglio

America and post-Soviet Russia square off underwater.

Beside being one of the best submarine movies ever made, Tony Scott's *Crimson Tide* also offers a succinct précis of the basic principles of nuclear deterrence. When a Russian nuclear missile installation is captured by a group of rebels, a US Navy nuclear submarine is sent to stand in position, ready for a pre-emptive strike. The belligerent captain, played by an impeccable Gene Hackman, has little regard for the world-ending potential of any one nuclear missile being fired — if he could, he would just press the big red button and be done with it. To his great chagrin, such a button does not exist, and every decision needs the approval of the Lieutenant Commander, a young Denzel Washington in one of his more subdued roles. The old-school pride and blinkered egocentrism of the Hackman clan finds itself consistently undermined throughout the film by Washington's more "complicated" and large-scale considerations. In an awe-inspiring sequence, what starts as casual banter between members of the crew unexpectedly builds up to a heart-stoppingly tense and terrifying conclusion, with Washington stating: "In the nuclear world, the true enemy can't be destroyed... The true enemy is war itself." Such scenes masterfully set up the film's unusually realistic and vertiginous stakes, which make the mutiny on board all the more engaging. It's exciting to have a '90s action film actively undermine the usual machismo of war movies, and offer a more reasonable approach to conflict. It is thrilling to see that clash of ideas embodied by an aging, angry white man in an ominous red hat, pitted against a young, well-spoken, educated black man – and to witness the latter win ◎

Elena is a French freelance film writer and editor based in London.

THE YES MEN FIX the world

Two merry pranksters pose as VIPs in order to hold a mirror up to corporate evildoing.

I'd show this audience the Bhopal film by the Yes Men. I loved it. It shows that campaigning films can be fun, but also very sad. Also, I think they were incredibly brave. Plus they don't seem to get embarrassed, which feels apt.

Kim Longinotto is a maker of excellent documentaries, her most recent being 2015's Dreamcatcher.

Directed by The Yes Men, 2009
Words by Kim Longinotto, Type by Laurène Boglio

Passport TO PIMLICO

What would happen if a national border was placed smack dab in the middle of London?

When the world has seemingly 'gawn barmey', a simple story of a plucky community coming together against 'The Man', setting out on their own but finally succumbing to the socialism that's better for everyone. One of my mum's favourite films so it must be good. A delightful romp.

Laurie is Ben Wheatley's regular cinematographer, but does work for other people too.

Directed by Henry Cornelius, 1949
Words by Laurie Rose, Type by Laurène Boglio

Curing the American Depression with a dance of death.

Half the world suffering from desperation or feeling cheated. The other half take advantage of that fact, for money, for fun or self relief. The rest probably ignore the whole thing. Picture yourself in the movie, let us know who you are. Careful, change the point of view, you may be on or off the dance floor.

Laia Costa is an actor from Barcelona who played the lead in Sebastian Schipper's one-take wonder, Victoria, *and will soon be seen in Dan Fogelman's* Life Itself *and Harry Wootliff's* Only You.

Directed by Sydney Pollack, 1969
Words by Laia Costa, Type by Laurène Boglio

This film, in all its glory, attacks the global negative narrative of who we are as a people.

Gina Prince-Bythewood is a filmmaker who directed Love and Basketball *and* The Secret Life of Bees.

Directed by Ryan Coogler, 2018
Words by Gina Prince-Bythewood, Type by Laurène Boglio

20 June –
1 July 2018
Programme Launch 23 May

ed
film
fest

#edfilmfest
edfilmfest.org.uk

EDINBURGH INTERNATIONAL
FILM FESTIVAL

REVIEWS CONTENTS

Words by **MATTHEW THRIFT**   Illustration by **SOPHIE MO**

Lucrecia Martel

It took the best part of a decade to bring *Zama* to the big screen. Its writer/director tells us about her epic journey.

It's been nine long years since the release of *The Headless Woman*, the previous feature from one of the leading lights of the new wave of Argentine cinema, Lucrecia Martel. Having spent almost two years on an aborted adaptation of graphic novel, 'El Eternauta', she turned her attention to Antonio di Benedetto's 'Zama', one of the key works of mid-century Argentine literature. Following a difficult, protracted production, the film finally premiered at the 2017 Venice Film Fesival. To say it's been worth the wait would be underselling one of the great cinematic achievements of the decade. We sat down with the master filmmaker to talk adaptation, representation and cinema's moral obligations.

LWLies: What can you tell us about the aborted science fiction film you were working on before *Zama*? Martel: The interesting thing about that project was the way that it enabled me to think about time and how best to represent it. Because that film didn't happen, I had all these ideas about time when I came to read *Zama*. I want to say this because I think it's important for producers to know: when a writer is contracted to write a script, they don't write it up in periods accorded by money. So someone asks you if you want to make a film, and that very same day you get immersed in the project, then more and more so as each day goes by.

It must be heartbreaking when a project falls apart having spent so long on it. Are you able to be philosophical about such instances? It was very tough indeed. The conflict in that project was over money, but then it's never really over money; it was about trust and about the idea. Underneath everything it was finally about a lack of trust from the director in the producer's work, and a lack of trust from the producer in the director's work. The script of *El Eternauta* ended with the survivors of the mission travelling up the Paraná River to Asunción, which is what I did. To escape from *El Eternauta*, I took a boat upriver – an old wooden boat, wholly inadequate for the journey. I wanted to reach Asunción too, but I didn't. On that boat, I read Zama. At the start of the book there's this image of a monkey coming and going with the flow of the river. It's an image, I think, that really reflects the writing style of di Benedetto. I don't know how it is in the English translation, but many times as you're reading, you find yourself having to go back to re-read passages, so it's like you're always going backwards and forwards.

Science fiction seems to have bled into *Zama* in an abstract sense. It's historical fiction but also somewhat alien, almost out of time. If we stop and think about it for a minute, a film about the past is really science fiction. When we think about what science fiction is as a genre, it's about technological development in the future, but the basis for that technology is in the present. So we imagine a potential future development in sci-fi, but our chances of being right about that are based on where we are right now. It's the same with the past. The most tangible thing about the past is what we did ourselves, and we know what that was. The present is what is left of our past. If we want to project far back into the past, it's the same process of imagination as looking into the future. I would even say that history is more arbitrary than science fiction, because history is written according to what you want it to show. For example, the history of Latin America is written by colonialists, it was written by those who were abusing their power in order to serve their own interests. There's proof of this today in all Latin American countries. They believe themselves to be modern democracies, and yet not one of them has an indigenous population that isn't living in abject poverty.

So what's the process of deciding what you're going to include, omit or embellish when it comes to your historical research? What I decided, with a certain degree of common sense, was that it wasn't possible for the slaves and servants to spend the entire time being submissive. No one, not even in Guantanamo, spends their entire time being submissive. I always thought it was curious that period dramas always showed extremes of submission or extremes of rebellion, there was no in-between. I think there is a state which we see today, where people who are economically and socially repressed lack belief or faith in the power that is oppressing them. So I applied common sense to it, imagining a people who don't always comply with this oppression, more like it was a state of conspiracy. That was the idea, and with a few details you can get it across. Given the tone of the film is one of absurd humour – it's not a serious work about heroes of the past – it was easier to get that across.

Do you think your take on the character of Zama is more sympathetic than di Benedetto's? No, but I think they're different. In di Benedetto there are many aspects to the character of Zama. I took some of them, but in the film there are various aspects to the character that can move you. Any summary of the actor or protagonist neglects all the individual messages the body receives in response to the character. An actor is an organism, and the capacity they have to communicate that is enormous, in ways that are not necessarily there in the book.

"I still don't know how to go about filming a rape scene without humiliating the woman in some way."

You omitted some of his more diabolical acts from the novel, the rape scene for instance. That scene was actually going to be in the film, but in the novel there are a number of scenes that work only in relation to each other. That was one, and there was another in which he had to sleep with someone in order to get some money. In the end, we didn't have the money to include one of those scenes, and if I wasn't going to include one, then I couldn't include the other. In any case, I still don't know how to go about filming a rape scene without humiliating the woman in some way. Twenty-five times every hour, you hear about a woman who's been abused or killed by her partner, her ex or her family for sexual reasons. We're all deeply troubled by this phenomenon of femicide we have in Argentina. I don't want to see this problem because I don't want to depict it – you don't want to turn a blind eye to it – just that if you want to have a serious discussion about it, you have to find a way of doing it without somehow implicitly endorsing it, or satisfying any hidden curiosity to see it.

Do you find that cinema often neglects its moral responsibility when it comes to depicting acts of violence? It's one of the most difficult things to talk about in this industry. You get a lot of North American films, right back from the time of the westerns, where they depict a binary split between the forces of good and the forces of evil. Evil depicted as massacring Indians, or Nazis, or Russians. In order to bolster this discourse, these films show images of war that demonstrate how awful they were, with the United States positioning themselves as a benevolent force in pursuit of war for the good of humankind. A discourse against those who wage war then becomes a justification for war. It's senseless.

Today what we're getting is a real effort from the West to depict the true enemy as Islamic terrorism, and again we're going down the wrong path. The answer, the response to violence has become yet more violence. It's very important to talk about, because today we're building up this 'enemy', who in certain respects consolidates this image through their actions, but I don't think that after any terrorist attack we have in London, for example, there is any serious thought about all the violence that is exacted upon Eurasia, Asia Minor or Africa. The only thoughts are how to bolster security and level more attacks against them. It's awful, because we're building up this huge lie that Islamic terrorism is so awful because it targets innocent civilians, which is almost justifying the idea that if a war is waged between soldiers, and only soldiers are killed in the firing line, then that's somehow legitimate.

And art is just as culpable as the media in its representation, presumably? It's an idea that I think everyone contributes to. We are all responsible for this. I really can't understand how we can't see that a terrorist attack is no different from a bombing of terrorists. All of these serve to kill people. It's the same thing. What we've done is create the notion that anyone of Arabic descent or origin is seen in the image of terrorism, the incarnation of terrorism, while if we see a western soldier, the image we have is one of protection, of security. But anything a soldier has on them is they're only either to kill or protect themselves. In the West, we're losing freedom to a certain extent, because now if I walk through London or other touristy places, I feel scared. While in the past, wars would be waged elsewhere, now they're coming on to home turf. We're getting a sense of what this feels like. Fear is being brought to us, which was something we previously didn't have to face. It used to be a feeling exclusively for the lands we went to colonise, but now we're being forced to face up to it ourselves, and we're not learning from it.

Do you tackle these questions of representation and responsibility in the filmmaking masterclasses you regularly hold? What I try to do in those workshops is let people see the limitations of their way of thinking, and to help them find tools to disrupt or subvert these ways of seeing the world that they've learned. Many people are numbed by their own perceptions, because it's actually quite useful for us as people to not be quite so aware of the way we think. I want them to be able to see injustices in the world that are dressed up as something else. Questions of representation are of course an issue, but more so, even, is perception. If you were to sharpen your perception, then representation would become much more interesting. Which is why it's so important how we choose to represent Islam, for example, because we're using the same ingredients we've always used, the same ingredients that led to the great wars of the past ◉

MUBI PRESENTS

ANGELA SCHANELEC SHOWING WITHOUT TELLING

PASSING SUMMER

MARSEILLE

AFTERNOON

ORLY

THE DREAMED PATH

RETROSPECTIVE NOW SHOWING ON MUBI.COM

Co-funded by the European Union
Creative Europe
With the support of Creative Europe - MEDIA Programme of the European Union

MUBI

Zama

Directed by
LUCRECIA MARTEL
Starring
DANIEL GIMÉNEZ CACHO
LOLA DUEÑAS
MATHEUS NACHTERGAELE
Released
25 MAY

ANTICIPATION.
Through the god damn roof. 2008's
The Headless Woman is a masterpiece.

ENJOYMENT.
Bewitching. With every edit comes a
surprise. Need to see it again, and fast.

IN RETROSPECT.
Hard to suppress the hyperbole with this one.
Truly an awesome achievement.

In 2016 the American publishing imprint *New York Review Books* released a timely translation of a 1956 Argentine novel named 'Zama' by the author Antonio di Benedetto. Timely in that at helpfully preceded the release of a much touted film adaptation by the staggeringly talented director Lucrecia Martel. Reading the book in anticipation of the film, two thoughts occurred: one, that this abrasive study of a disconsolate, cock-blocked political functionary trapped in the crumbling South American outpost of Asunción, Paraguay during the late 18th century, is surely, in the West, to be considered a lost literary classic; and two, that transforming it into a film is an impossible endeavour, as the text is largely formed of circuitous, self-abasing inner monologue. In short, it's some really gnarly shit.

But we all know that the cinematic masterworks which endure over time are those forged from tougher material, and so it is with Martel's astonishing, intuitive and desperately sad new comedy. Her adaptation – lightly abridged but thematically perhaps more expansive – maintains Zama's pitiful sexual neediness, but emphasises his story as a cautionary tale of colonial misadventure. Our hapless hero's futile station is teased in the film's opening shot as Zama, smartly turned out in official military threads and tricorn hat, strikes a mighty pose on a shoreline and glances out to sea. His desire for escape and autonomy is palpable, but so is the sense that he is, like Antoine Doinel at the end of *The 400 Blows*, standing at the edge of the world with nowhere to go but backwards.

In the lead role is Daniel Giménez Cacho, whose tamped-down and softly expressive performance perfectly transmits Zama's barely concealed astonishment at his endless run of bad luck. Every element of the film conspires to mock his lowly stature, from where he's placed in the frame (often locked to one of its edges) to the symphony of chirps and tweets which emanate from the backdrop and ally his actions to those of local fauna. There is a sequence in which he is in the middle of an altercation with a co-functionary. As he talks, a llama wanders into the room, stops next to him, looks around, and then wanders out again. Cacho manages not to flinch, playing the moment as just another surreal interlude in this lawless outland where man and beast are largely interchangeable. One beast who is the subject of much contemplation, however, is the elusive bogeyman known as Vicuña Porto, a figure whose murderous antics are causing vital blockages on the trade routes between nearby townships. Attempts to track and kill the elusive Porto appear to be the cause of the administrative disarray.

The loose-leaf plotting sees Zama attempt to secure a written permission to return home to his wife and children, thereby fulfilling the masculine ideal of family man and protector. Duty aside, his all-pervasive sexual longing leads him to spy on a circle of bathing beauties and also attempt to seduce the cigar-smoking, acid-tongued treasurer's daughter, Luciana Piñares de Luenga, played as a boisterous man-eater by the always wonderful Spanish actor Lola Dueñas. His laughable attempts at playing away are hampered by his earnest charm, and Cacho, through his performance, manages to beautifully stress Zama's limits as both a bureaucrat and an amorous dandy. This deplorable figure eventually catches sight of his own deficiencies as a human, and retreats towards the warm embrace of certain death in the film's quixotic closing chapter.

In the spirit of its chaotic setting, the story is unfurled as a calypso-soundtracked stream-of-consciousness, a rustic dream state which reflects the notion that Zama himself is reacting to the moment rather than executing some carefully devised political masterplan. In the end, the film is about a man who sells his soul by the increment as he eventually realises he's alone in the world. It also suggests that those carrying out the imperialist dictates of a home nation are naturally drawn to exploitation, as if it's the only way to exert political power. He hates having to ask other people to help him lest it undermine his middling title. He also likes to milk his status for all its worth, especially when it comes to "helping" his female maids or the indigenous locals who clearly despise his presence.

Even though the film is set centuries ago, there's something futuristic, maybe even post-apocalyptic, about the frazzled, comically unfair world that Martel manufactures. Zama is an unexceptional man, a drone in many respects. Yet Martel is supremely empathetic in her depiction of this person who is tempted by selfish impulse but rejected by the world around him. Maybe because, until the very end, he is seduced by the notion of hope and the touching belief that he will be saved by his cohorts before it's too late. Only in beating his addiction to hope does he eventually find the transcendence and escape that he craves.
DAVID JENKINS

Pandora's Box (1929)

Directed by
GW PABST
Starring
LOUISE BROOKS
FRITZ KORTNER
FRANCIS LEDERER
Released
10 JULY

ANTICIPATION.
Lulu returns to the big screen.

ENJOYMENT.
*Reaffirms its classic status.
Still one of the most iconic
performances in early cinema.*

IN RETROSPECT.
*If this is, for whatever reason, still
on your "must see" list, take this
chance to tick it off.*

Only a cocktail of happenstance, gumption, and raw talent could provide the jet fuel required to propel a raven-haired starlet from a dusty Kansas cowtown to the movie palaces and cabarets of Weimar-era Berlin. Call it the Lulu effect, after the diminutive bestowed upon Louise Brooks (more on that later), whose meteoric rise and too-familiar fall have captivated film historians for decades. Born to an "artistic" family, the bulk of Brooks' early training was in the burgeoning practice of modern dance, but after clocking time in the chorus line she made a *pleia* for the big screen. Her career was regretfully brief, but her resulting filmography – and myriad ways in which she changed screen acting – cannot be overstated.

After a few years of kicking around Hollywood playing flappers and sundry other 'good-time gals' in the sidelines, Brooks hightailed it to Europe, and began the legendary collaboration that would make her an icon. *Pandora's Box* was the first film made with pioneering Expressionist director Georg Wilhelm Pabst, and it was an altogether new kind of melodrama. The film was adapted from a stage play, but possesses a strictly cinematic vocabulary that was heretofore unseen within the young medium. In mighty close-ups and lingering glances at his characters' gestures or hair's-width head turns, Pabst commanded full use of the screen space that an orchestra seat-vantage could only hint at. And it's his caressing photography of Brooks, especially, that provides a deeply human foundation to an otherwise play-by-play story of a fallen woman clawing her way back up to the stars.

Under the strong arm of Pabst's direction, Brooks' performance blossoms beyond cliche into a bouquet of learned strength – *Herr Direktor* uses her vulnerability and softness in one scene, exploits her nonchalance and steely resolve in the next. And Brooks meets her brilliant svengali halfway, imbuing her role as a bespoiled ingenue with a hard-earned, authentic worldliness. All of 22 when the film was made, she had already seen more of the world than many of us could hope to in a thousand lifetimes. By the time she arrived at Pabst's Berlin studio, she had already had her fill of guileless American comedies and the assembly-line studios that churned them out like T-model Fords.

True to life, Brooks plays Lulu, a former dancer who – in the words of her old friend and likely former pimp – has "made good for herself" as the kept woman of a wealthy, older Jewish newspaper editor. With folding money aplenty and bottles of sherry ever handy, Lulu is a natural mark for an old friend – that odious, aforementioned procurer – whose arrival at her penthouse love nest sets off a series of mishaps and misunderstandings that come to spell tragedy for our flitting heroine. When sugar-daddy Schön is forced to make a good marriage, Lulu's station in life is the first casualty. "You'll have to kill me to get rid of me," she swoons, and in so doing invites upon herself the mark of Cain. It's a pity safety and comfort are not among the shortlist of life's guarantees, for though Lulu is in the catbird seat today, we know what misery lays in wait for her tomorrow.
CAROLINE GOLUM

"A CINEMATIC MARVEL"

MANOHLA DARGIS,
THE NEW YORK TIMES

★★★★★
**"A STRANGE,
SENSUAL WONDER...
ASTONISHING"**

XAN BROOKS, THE GUARDIAN

★★★★★
**"BEWITCHING...
TRULY AN AWESOME
ACHIEVEMENT"**

DAVID JENKINS, LITTLE WHITE LIES

ZAMA

A film by LUCRECIA MARTEL

IN CINEMAS MAY 25

new wave films   WWW.NEWWAVEFILMS.CO.UK

The Ciambra

Directed by **JONAS CARPIGNANO**
Starring **PIO AMATO, KOUDOUS SEIHON, DAMIANO AMATO**
Released **15 JUNE**

Director Jonas Carpignano broke through on the festival circuit in 2015 with *Mediterranea*, a tale of two refugees making their way from Africa to southern Italy. He returns to the latter environment with follow-up feature *The Ciambra*, an expansion of a 2014 short, which attempts to present a portrait of another marginalised group with a similar degree of verisimilitude: in this case, a small Romani community in the Italian region of Calabria.

His approach towards realism not only involves shooting on handheld 16mm in a vérité documentary style and populating his cast with mostly non-professional actors. It also includes many of his lead performer's actual family as members of his on-screen household. Fourteen-year-old Pio (Pio Amato) is that central character, a young man in a hurry to grow up; freely smoking and drinking, presenting an outwardly cocksure exterior, yet terrified to talk to a girl he likes. He follows his older brother, Cosimo (Damiano Amato), everywhere, picking up the tricks of the various hustling trades required to survive on the streets of their hometown. When his role model sibling is suddenly imprisoned by police, and his father also taken in, Pio takes up the mantle of head of the family. His unusual ease with sliding between the region's various factions – fellow Romani, local Italians and African immigrants – proves useful at first, but his increasingly dangerous criminal actions attract unwelcome attention.

If these coming-of-age story points sound familiar, Carpignano is at least careful not to overplay any of his narrative beats, though a certain turn in the third act depends on a big convenience that's a little hard to swallow. That said, the writer-director has a real gift for a sense of place and this largely works in creating a vivid portrait of this region. So much so that you almost wishe it would step outside Pio's point of view to let us get to know some of the supporting players more. **JOSH SLATER-WILLIAMS**

ANTICIPATION. *Italy's submission for Best Foreign Language Film at the Oscars just gone.* **3**

ENJOYMENT. *Mostly solid, though lacking some urgency in its near two hour runtime.* **3**

IN RETROSPECT. *The textures and attention to detail enrich the familiar story beats.* **3**

The Dreamed Path

Directed by **ANGELA SCHANELEC**
Starring **MIRIAM JAKOB, THORBJÖRN BJÖRNSSON, MAREN EGGERT**
Released **10 MAY**

The German director Angela Schanelec has the ability to make an innocuous shot of water being poured into a glass appear like a scorching nuclear explosion at the centre of the frame. Her camera is used as a tool to elevate banal action to the level of dance or poetry, where she appears less interested in physical actions and their consequences, and more in the primal visual beauty of the movement itself. *The Dreamed Path* is her 11th feature and any attempt to offer a succinct plot précis would be a foolish endeavour indeed. It begins with a couple badly singing a cover of 'The Lion Sleeps Tonight' and being handsomely rewarded for their efforts by passers by. As Greek activists celebrate their country's entry into the EU in the adjacent carpark, the man (Thorbjörn Björnsson) receives a phone call and discovers his mother is in hospital. He breaks down and then the couple swiftly part ways.

The film then takes on the form of a lucid reverie as the story comprises of short interludes which are almost like reaction shots to a stimulus we don't see (or, perhaps, are invited to imagine). The actors speak in clipped, over-enunciated parlance as if they're hypnotised and it's rare that a question will receive a conventional response. The action, which takes us to a hospice, swimming baths, a school, the set of a weird rustic cop show and the entrance of a suburban U-bahn station in Berlin, skits and flits between decades, introduces new characters at random and is evasive when it comes to anything resembling an obvious meaning. Yet a puzzle with many of the pieces missing can produce its own distinctive and alternative image, and *The Dreamed Path* does just that. Schanelec's work is currently enjoying a full retrospective on MUBI, where you'll also be able to catch this puzzling, but captivating new one. **DAVID JENKINS**

ANTICIPATION. *Schanelec is a big name in the more rarified corners of the festival circuit.* **3**

ENJOYMENT. *It somehow manages to be boring and exciting at the same time. Which is exciting.* **4**

IN RETROSPECT. *Its oblique beauty is more evident on a second watch.* **4**

Racer and the Jailbird

Directed by **MICHAËL R ROSKAM**
Starring **MATTHIAS SCHOENAERTS,**
ADÈLE EXARCHOPOULOS, ERIC DE STAERCKE
Released **13 JULY**

In its native Belgian, Michaël R Roskam's latest feature was titled *Le Fidèle* (The Faithful), which is fairly alright as far as movie names go. In the crazy world of international film distribution and title translation, this evolved into the rather clunky *Racer and the Jailbird*. This naff nomenclature serves as a warning as effective as the signage above Dante's apocryphal Inferno: "Abandon hope all ye who enter here."

It stars Adèle Exarchopoulos as Bibi, the eponymous Racer, and Matthias Schoenaerts as Gigi, the Jailbird. The pair meet and – at breakneck speed – fall in love. At this point the story diverges into three parts which chart their romance, Gigi's exploits as a Belgian bank robber, and the aftermath in which a heist goes spectacularly awry. Things descend into morose melodrama from then on, as Bibi pines for Gigi and becomes embroiled with gangsters in misguided attempts to free her incarcerated lover. All the while, Gigi skulks around looking glum.

It's an insipid tale which takes plot inspiration from the likes of petrolhead antics of Nicolas Winding Refn's *Drive* and David Lynch's *Wild at Heart,* but lacks any of the ambition and creativity which propelled those films to greatness. The weak script offers little in the way of character development for its two central players, and manages to include more sex scenes than chances for Bibi to display any facet of her personality that doesn't revolve around her ne'er-do-well fiancé. A spectacularly stupid third-act twist undermines the rest of the plot, and given how little character development is offered beyond a few laboured dog metaphors that hint at Gigi's troubled upbringing, there's no reason to really care about the peril facing the couple. Painfully serious and unintentionally silly, this is self-indulgent filmmaking at its worst, and a frustratingly boring attempt at reinventing the neo-noir wheel.
HANNAH WOODHEAD

ANTICIPATION. *Director Roskam's*
The Drop and Haun *weren't bad.* **3**

ENJOYMENT. *Matthias and Adele don't*
look like they're enjoying themselves. **2**

IN RETROSPECT. *A car crash. And not the*
Cronenberg *kind.* **2**

A Cambodian Spring

Directed by **CHRISTOPHER KELLY**
Released **18 MAY**

The residents of Boeung Kak, a lakeside suburb of Phnom Penh, sob as bulldozers demolish their houses. This scene, captured by the Irish director Chris Kelly in his documentary *A Cambodian Spring*, is typical of the development sweeping the eponymous east Asian country. Hun Sen, the world's most overlooked despot, became prime minister in 1985 and has spent his three decades in power, quietly selling off land and natural resources – often without public consent.

The makers of the film spent six years following three activists resisting this steamroller approach to development. The evictees living next to Boeung Kak lake organised behind two residents, Tep Vanny and Toul Srey Pov, who blossomed from shy stay-at-home mothers to megaphone-touting warriors. Meanwhile a Buddhist monk, Venerable Loun Sovath, helps advocate for his parishioners despite calls from the government-linked Buddhist regulatory body to stay out of politics. Kelly's cinematography finds a brooding, doomed beauty in the landscape. He isn't afraid to stray beyond the familiar narrative of the heroic everyman taking on powerful corporations. The already tragic film reaches peak despair while documenting the activists' ugly infighting and it works at documenting the raw actuality of these skirmishes. But it feels as though the powerful people responsible for causing the anguish remain where they want to be – in the shadows. The withholding of context and backstories can also leave some important points tantalisingly vague.

The film ends shortly after the 2013 elections, when opposition supporters took to the streets in cheering, hopeful droves. In the five years since that near-defeat at the polls, Hun Sen has outlawed all protest, jailed the opposition leader and banned his party. Instead of documenting the shoots of a democratic uprising, *A Cambodian Spring* lays witness to the beginning of an ugly new era. **EVE WATLING**

ANTICIPATION. *The dramatic protests surrounding*
the 2013 Cambodian elections remain under-explored. **3**

ENJOYMENT. *Emotions run high as grassroots*
activists protest land-grabs and police shootings. **4**

IN RETROSPECT. *An in-the-mix glimpse at a moment*
of hope, which leaves unanswered questions. **4**

Jeune Femme

Directed by
LÉONOR SERRAILLE
Starring
**LAETITIA DOSCH
SOULEYMANE SEYE NDIAYE
GRÉGOIRE MONSAINGEON**
Released
18 MAY

ANTICIPATION.
Going in totally blind here.

ENJOYMENT.
*Laetitia Dosch is
breathtakingly charismatic.
You can't take your eyes off
her, even on repeat viewings*

IN RETROSPECT.
*A character study, a feminist
awakening, and a piquant comedy
all wrapped in one.*

We first meet Paula with a giant bandage on her forehead, covering the wound caused by headbutting her ex-boyfriend's door. She has just been turfed out of his Parisian flat, where he works as a well-known photographer and she, presumably, pads around like a spoiled housepet. Léonor Serraille's debut feature film gently probes female identity and the smothering influence of the 'genius' male, and does so with all but the slightest imposition from the man himself. Paula, instead, is the sole focus of *Jeune Femme*.

Laetitia Dosch stars as the lost thirtysomething who has to regain her sense of self after serving as an artist's muse for a decade, and her performance is magnetic. Words tumble from her mouth at speed, her red hair flies in her face, and she's a constant whirling dervish of energetic feeling. But the truth is, Paula doesn't have a very deep sense of self. Post-breakup, she is broke, homeless, and directionless after being unceremoniously replaced by a younger girl. She rubs people up the wrong way, she's unqualified for most jobs, and even her mother is estranged from her. As the film progresses, Serraille follows Paula as she searches for work and attempts to figure out her place in the world on her own terms. Along the way, she steals her ex's fluffy white cat, befriends a girl through a bizarre misunderstanding, becomes a loving but irresponsible au pair and attempts to patch up her relationship with her mother.

With the manic energy of its lead performance left to speak for itself, Serraille's style is one of confident realism. There are run-down hotels, lonely public parks and unfriendly rain-soaked streets: Paris here is an ugly, overwhelming metropolis, with no residue of its romantic reputation. Ousmane, a security guard who befriends Paula, is the only character who can still see and believes in the old Paris. He's an immigrant, and from his outsider's eye, he sees the city's appeal. To Paula, who once was ensnared within its artistic and financial limelight, it's less attractive. Serraille directed *Jeune Femme* while pregnant, and when similar topics arise in the movie, Paula's strangely intimate conversation with a female doctor feels strikingly genuine. The crew of the film was populated mostly by women, perhaps giving an empathetic backdrop for its actors to perform against. And while Paula does make an unsteady trajectory towards financial and sexual freedom, the path is never clear. Her personality – brash, emotional, mouthy – is unchanged, giving a further tinge of reality to the film's proceedings. With its reminders of how arduously slow growing up can really be, the film is like a long-overdue coming-of-age story. Even if Paula is 31.

Yet *Jeune Femme* is also drolly funny, as when Paula joins a tyrannically feminine retail team in a shopping mall lingerie bar. Slightly unhinged though she may be, there's a warmth and determination in Paula that's difficult not to like. She's a grown woman in a state of arrested development, but she loves fiercely and learns independence in a piecemeal, occasionally painful way. Serraille's film is one of the most satisfying and gently feminist character studies of recent times, using as its guiding light the sheer force of personality of its lead.
CHRISTINA NEWLAND

Interview by **DAVID JENKINS** *Illustration by* **SOPHIE MO**

Laetitia Dosch

Following her scintllating turn in *Jeune Femme,* we meet a French superstar in the making.

If some top level cat interactions were not enough, then you must see Léonor Serraille's *Jeune Femme* for the breakout lead performance by the French actor Laetitia Dosch. We met her in Paris where she told us her theories about acting and offered details of her past life as a film critic.

LWLies: Could you describe the first meeting you had with Léonor? Dosch: Okay, Léonor wrote me a letter. It's the first real letter I've received for a job. A very long letter, with the script included. I was so moved by that. I read the script, and it was extremely well written and it was a part I had been waiting for years to play. So powerful, complex, different shades and also I loved the... politically, it was a very left wing film, and I loved that. There's something very delicate about Léonor. She's quite shy. This is exactly what I need to work well because it's very reassuring. So we talked, and she was shy, and I was shy because she was shy. But we knew from the moment we met each other that we should work together.

Why do you see the film as left leaning? The rebellious element. It talks about people who have several jobs to survive and also people whose values are more important than work. The idea of meeting someone new and different. Looking at the sun.

Do you think it's a feminist film? I think so. Because first she is an object and she then becomes a subject. So, yes, it's feminist, but Léonor is quite cautious with this kind of term. It was very important for her that the character had many faces, because she thinks, in real life, women are like that.

You are someone who has worked a lot in the theatre. What are the differences between stage acting and screen acting? You know, stage acting is so difficult because every night you have to be as good or better than the night before. It's very difficult but I like that – it's healthy because you don't take anything for granted. Also, the way of working really depends on the director. It's not a question of stage or cinema, it's a question of the direction. Sometimes they want you to improvise, sometimes they want you as you, sometimes they want you to be very precise, sometimes they want you to work more with your body. You have to be more precise with your body. Paula is very physical. She's moves in a certain way. She has a link to objects. This interaction with objects comes from the theatre, I think. But when I'm on stage I try, sometimes, to imagine I have a camera very near me so I can concentrate and not overplay.

Is it true that you write criticism as well? Not really. I wrote criticism, but I'm not really doing that any more because other people are doing that. And I'm so happy that they're doing that. I wrote about actors because I thought that people were not talking enough. The critics were not that good at talking about actors, not that precise. What actors do is beautiful, so I thought, okay I'm going to write about actors.

What were they not talking about? It's like judgement, saying like he's good or not good. It's not precise so I was sad about that. I started to write for this reason. I wrote about Julianne Moore and Emmanuelle Devos.

And why did you stop writing? Because it's so exhausting. I had to see all these films. I saw ten films with one actor in over a single day. Seeing a film and then you have to write to find the thesis... oh no, I can't do that, I can't do your job.

Was it a learning process for you? Yes, for sure. The way actors move, the way they... Julianne Moore, she's so amazing with her hands, for instance. She's very sweet.

Is directing something you're thinking about as well? Right now, I'm directing a new play, I'm writing and directing plays and then I would like to write with someone. That's what I would like to do, to write a script with someone else. That would be nice.

Would you be keen to work with Léonor again? Yes. I also would like to write with her. I'd like that. If I acted for again, it would also take me less time to memorise the script ◎

The Endless

Directed by
JUSTIN BENSON
AARON MOORHEAD
Starring
CALLIE HERNANDEZ
EMILY MONTAGUE
JAMES JORDAN
Released
29 JUNE

ANTICIPATION.
I want to believe that sci-fi can be realised on a shoestring budget.

ENJOYMENT.
The truth is out there, but not in these patchy performances.

IN RETROSPECT.
Trust no one who tells you they can write, direct, produce, act, shoot and edit.

"I rescued us from a cult. I saved you from mass suicide. You're welcome," says Justin (Justin Benson) to his brother Aaron (Aaron Moorhead), in the opening minutes of *The Endless*. Straight out of the gate, this two-man creative team (they have also written, directed, produced, shot and edited the film) lets you know what they're all about: masculine posturing, earnest chat and saying the word 'cult' a lot. But as *The Endless* progresses, the pair prove to be shooting for the stars – on an indie budget, no less – with their lo-fi sci-fi thriller about religion, faith, memory, fate and family.

ICYMI, Justin and Aaron fled from a 'UFO death cult' as teens. (Don't worry. They'll mention it, well, endlessly). Ten years later, when a VHS tape from the sect arrives on their doorstep, the brothers are impelled to call upon the desert commune once more. Revisiting the home they left behind sparks unrest between the two, who jostle to find their place in the cult's pecking order. Supernatural events around the campsite intensify, and the cult prepares for imminent rapture.

It's a film that riffs on the subjectivity of perception from beneath a sci-fi glaze. With minimal use of special effects, and a great deal of dialogue, it's more a study of masculinity, leadership and human psychology. The curious premise and gradual revelations partially make up for the want of blockbuster production values. Attention is paid equally to story and character development – for the male leads, at least. (Anna, played by *Alien: Covenant*'s Callie Hernandez, likes to sew, while Kira Powell's Lizzy is a manic pixie drug girl.)

Though intriguing, the plot is puckered by confusion. Once resolved, it leaves behind more questions than answers – and in a frustrating, not stimulating, way. Similarly, the intended tone of some scenes is unclear, as when the brothers argue about whether women can be paedophiles. Exasperated, alpha Justin repeatedly tells junior Aaron, "Go to sleep," with such a comedic rhythm it seems like Benson, as actor and editor, is inexplicably playing the scene for laughs.

Some stylistic devices do land, such as Moorhead's voyeuristic cinematography. During their de-programming sessions, the brothers address the camera directly. When they're alone in remote San Diego scrub, the camera appears to stalk them. It takes on a will of its own. These flourishes sit well in a film about ways of seeing and being seen. Even the film's unseen monster – an invisible entity that communicates through tangible imagery – could be read as the embodiment of genre cinema's own big bad: the male gaze. Though it's questionable whether this was the directors' intention.

The pair do seem keen on building their own cinematic universe, though. Justin and Aaron (the characters) first appeared in 2012 as anonymous 'UFO Cult Members' in Benson and Moorhead's debut feature *Resolution*. Likewise, the leads from that flick show up here, in a self-satisfied aside of intertextual showboating. Holistic creative control might be top priority for this ambitious twosome, but an objective pair of eyes on the script might have propelled *The Endless* from acceptable to stellar.
AIMEE KNIGHT

VOTED TOP FESTIVAL
BY BBC 6 MUSIC LISTENERS

GREEN MAN

★★★★★ THE GUARDIAN   ★★★★★ THE TIMES

2018

16-19 AUGUST. BRECON BEACONS. WALES

THE WAR ON DRUGS · FLEET FOXES · KING GIZZARD & THE LIZARD WIZARD

JOHN GRANT · GRIZZLY BEAR · DIRTY PROJECTORS

THE BRIAN JONESTOWN MASSACRE · TEENAGE FANCLUB
THE BLACK ANGELS · PUBLIC SERVICE BROADCASTING
ANNA CALVI · CATE LE BON · MOUNT KIMBIE · FLOATING POINTS (SOLO LIVE)
JOHN MAUS · BAXTER DURY · JOAN AS POLICE WOMAN · THE LEMON TWIGS
TELEMAN · COURTNEY MARIE ANDREWS · KEVIN MORBY
SUSANNE SUNDFOR · CURTIS HARDING · WHYTE HORSES
JANE WEAVER · TAMIKREST · JOHN TALABOT · BEAK> · WYE OAK
SIMIAN MOBILE DISCO (LIVE W/ DEEP THROAT CHOIR) · ALEX CAMERON
PHOEBE BRIDGERS · ROLLING BLACKOUTS COASTAL FEVER
GOAT GIRL · KING TUFF · FOLLAKZOID · KELLY LEE OWENS
THE LOVELY EGGS · TUNNG · BO NINGEN · CHASTITY BELT · HMLTD
LUCY DACUS · MARLON WILLIAMS · FRANKIE COSMOS · SWEET BABOO
JADE BIRD · A HAWK AND A HACKSAW · XYLOURIS WHITE · LOST HORIZONS
BOY AZOOGA · PICTISH TRAIL · THE KVB · OMNI · DUDS · SNAPPED ANKLES
SNAIL MAIL · AMBER ARCADES · BAS JAN · ED DOWIE · CHARLES WATSON
IDER · SHANNON LAY · HALEY HEYNDERICKX · WESTERMAN
SEAMUS FOGARTY · STELLA DONNELLY · JIM GHEDI · JUANITA STEIN
SACRED PAWS · SORRY · SPINNING COIN · J. BERNARDT · HORSEY
RISING: AADAE · ACCU · ADWAITH · BLACK MIDI · BUZZARD
THE COSMIC ARRAY · FENNE LILY · GROUP LISTENING · HAZE · SOCK

10 WILD LANDS OF LAUGHS, LITERATURE, ART, SCIENCE, FAMILY ADVENTURE AND MUSIC

TICKETS ON SALE NOW!
GREENMAN.NET

My Friend Dahmer

Directed by
MARC MEYERS
Starring
ROSS LYNCH
ALEX WOLFF
ANNE HECHE
Released
1 JUNE

ANTICIPATION.
Another irresponsible movie about a serial killer?

ENJOYMENT.
From mild ennui to utter terror and sorrow. Amazing.

IN RETROSPECT.
A unique entry into the serial killer movie genre, and one of the best.

At first glance, Marc Meyers' *My Friend Dahmer* looks like another serial killer movie playing into our morbid fascination with these incomprehensible figures. Set during the months leading up to notorious killer Jeffrey Dahmer's first murder, the film seems to promise an 'explanation' for his actions. Sure enough, Meyers faithfully reproduces known details of Dahmer's youth, in what can feel like little more than an adaptation of the 'early life' section of his Wikipedia profile. Raised by a mother with mental health issues and a father who did the best he could, Dahmer was unpopular at school, an awkward teen who chose to dissect roadkill rather than socialise with his classmates.

Things get more interesting when Dahmer abruptly finds himself with three new friends, including the easy-going John Backderf (played by the transcendent Alex Wolff), the boy who went on to write a graphic novel upon which the film is based. Far from pursuing sordid fame with juicy stories about the killer's youth, Backderf's work is animated by a need to grapple with a nagging sense of remorse: did his treatment of Dahmer contribute to his becoming a killer? Was there anything he could have done to stop him?

Dahmer's new friends do not appear in a particularly positive light. Their interest in him does not stem from genuine concern or sympathy. Rather, the weirdo attracts their attention when he simulates cerebral palsy in class, a disturbing joke which the kids latch onto as a last rebellious prank before college. They soon nickname this type of class-time disruption as 'doing a Dahmer.'

Following the boy, we are powerless witnesses to his frustration when he ultimately fails to get the sympathy he craves. His friends push the joke too far and then abandon him, and Dahmer's sense of alienation is a deeply relatable example of adolescent emotion. We've all felt how sadness can take on an existential dimension in the summer months, and when Jeffrey finds himself home alone in the middle of a warm afternoon while everyone else is preparing for graduation with their family, it is difficult not to feel his heartbreak.

But empathy has its limits. When Dahmer decides to turn his resentment into violence — and it is presented as a decision, not an impulse — we cannot follow him there. The pain we felt for his hopelessness becomes the sorrow of knowing that a kind word or gesture might have delayed his crimes, but not stopped them.

This profound sadness is the bedrock of a growing sense of fear, which reaches fever pitch intensity in an impressively executed set piece near the end of the film. After not speaking to him for weeks, Backderf offers Dahmer a ride back to his house, one last encounter before he goes to college and forever out of his friend's life. Almost unbearably terrifying, the confrontation restores to Dahmer the stomach-churning dread and misery that reading about serial killers often induces, but watching movies about them rarely does. Although *My Friend Dahmer* does not resolve the impossible question of 'nature vs. nurture', it approaches it with a humanity that is too often missing from such stories.
ELENA LAZIC

McQueen

Directed by
IAN BONHÔTE
PETER ETTEDGUI
Released
8 JUNE

ANTICIPATION.
Alexander McQueen was one of the greatest fashion designers ever and his life was fascinating.

ENJOYMENT.
Seeing how tightly McQueen's personal life was connected to his gorgeous and disturbing garments is often gobsmacking.

IN RETROSPECT.
A generous and mostly respectful approach to a beautifully complicated and unapologetically hungry man.

It is a touching tribute that composer Michael Nyman scored *McQueen*, the documentary about the celebrated and sorely missed British fashion designer, as he loved to listen to Nyman's orchestrations when working in his atelier. The film itself follows that taste for symphonies: in under two hours, directors Ian Bonhôte and Peter Ettedgui (the latter wrote the critically acclaimed Brando doc *Listen To Me Marlon*) speed through the blistering life and art of their subject. Even if they occasionally verge on indulgence, their relentless filmmaking mostly succeeds at evoking Alexander McQueen's passion, disarming generosity and eventual heart-wrenching downward spiralling.

McQueen's extravagance isn't a secret: "I pull these horrors out of my soul and put them on the catwalk," he tells a group of journalists. By focussing on the man, Bonhôte and Ettedgui aim to better understand the legend, providing a frame of reference for those iconically horrifying and beautiful outfits. Many of McQueen's closest friends/collaborators (fashion really was his whole life) give candid interviews to the camera, detailing how fascinatingly bizarre and kind he was. Returning frequently throughout the film to discuss the evolution of their relationships with the designer, these friends are also given a lot of space for their own personalities to shine through. Instead of turning its subject into a god-like elusive being (which post-mortem artist documentaries are always at a risk of doing), the directors highlight McQueen's humanity, framing those around him as being essential to building his identity.

An impressive amount of television and home movie footage from the time allows us see McQueen speak in his own words and behave naturally. Aged only 23 when his MA show at the prestigious Central St Martin's College of Art and Design put him on the map, the South London-born, working-class designer had a childishness and punk spirit that also came through in his work. This symbiosis between his jubilant personality and his outrageous creations explains his vertiginous rise to cult status, and the film reaches emotional highs when it revels in this magical formula: when McQueen watches robotic arms spray-paint a DIY dress for the splendid finale of his 1999 spring/summer show No. 13, his tears are also ours for they are so clearly the direct product of his eccentric mind and personal history.

McQueen mostly avoids didactic conjunctions between the designer's life and work. The film's structure into chapters, however, harms its otherwise unrestrained embracing of his complexity. Tacky CGI title cards show skulls covered with blooming then crumbling flowers which represent McQueen's rise and fall, and delineate periods in his life. On top of slowing down the exhilarating rhythm of such a full existence, this cheap narrative device is distasteful. McQueen had every right to compose his own departure as he pleased (he became obsessed with skulls in his later shows and fantasised about taking his own life on the catwalk). When Bonhôte and Ettedgui do so, and after the fact, they provide too neat a conclusion for a life so ill-suited to comfortable boundaries.
MANUELA LAZIC

Generation Wealth

Directed by
LAUREN GREENFIELD
Released
20 JULY

ANTICIPATION.
Greenfield's got a knack for fascinating subject matter.

ENJOYMENT.
Peppy and engaging, with a slick, Hollywood zeal.

IN RETROSPECT.
Afraid to cut deep and a little too conservative.

When Gordon Gecko declared "Greed is good" in 1987, a whole generation nodded along in reverential agreement. At the time, Oliver Stone's *Wall Street* was seen by the upper echelons less as a blistering indictment of unregulated capitalism, and more a style guide for the financial district elite. Though the halcyon days of the late '80s and early '90s have long-since passed, they hold a peculiar kind of fascination for documentarian Lauren Greenfield, who began her career over 25 years ago, recording the lifestyles of the rich and famous. *Generation Wealth* – her first film since 2012's *The Queen of Versailles* – is the culmination of a lifelong obsession with the obsessed.

As such, it makes sense that Greenfield chooses to turn the camera on herself and her family, interviewing her parents, husband and children about how her single-mindedness as an artist has impacted on their lives. At the same time, she reunites with previous subjects and old friends, including baby beauty queen Eden Wood, star of the hit reality show *Toddlers & Tiaras*, and FBI Most Wanted fraudster Florian Homm. Due to her personal rapport with her subjects, there's an easy candor to the interviews, the antithesis of Louis Theroux's awkward blustering. There's a sense that her charming subjects are chosen for their quotability: "Does Harvard Business School teach you to be a good person?" she asks Florian. He laughs before replying, "No, we're fine-tuned to rule the world."

There's a glossiness about *Generation Wealth* that makes it captivating to watch, reminiscent of Adam McKay's slick feature *The Big Short* for its snappy approach to explaining complex financial terms. But instead of focusing on the money, Greenfield is concerned with who has it and who doesn't. She speaks to rappers, celebrity offspring, a former porn star and an ex-girlfriend of Donald Trump turned Las Vegas party planner, examining the reality of what money can (and can't) buy. There's a slight triteness to all this, particularly the suggestion that the best things in life really are free, which is a belief that only ever seems to be held by those with money in the first place.

Looking past the twee examination of money's moral value, Greenfield provides a fascinating – albeit brief – look at the commodification of the American Dream, and its dissemination around the world. She visits a chipper Icelander, who went from fisherman to banker to fisherman, following the trajectory of his country's 2008-2011 financial crisis. Meanwhile, former Communist countries such as Russia and China, have rapidly embraced Capitalism and become leading consumers of Western luxury goods. In a film packed with fascinating lines of enquiry, these two moments in particular feels worthy of further examination, but despite its ambition, there's simply not enough time to cover it all.

This doesn't come as much of a surprise, given that this film feels so personal to Greenfield – it's less about wealth as a abstract concept and more her personal connection to it. Much like her photography work, *Generation Wealth* has all the surface appeal and charisma of a luxe coffee table book, but this documentary lacks the killer instinct to tell us, the Great Unwashed Masses, anything we don't already know about excess. **HANNAH WOODHEAD**

On Chesil Beach

Directed by
DOMINIC COOKE
Starring
SAOIRSE RONAN
BILLY HOWLE
ANNE-MARIE DUFF
Released
18 MAY

ANTICIPATION.
Saoirse Ronan is as close to a mark of quality as you can get these days.

ENJOYMENT.
An awkward adapation of an awkward novella.

IN RETROSPECT.
Attempts to take on Big Questions while also offering something for the tea-time crowd. Doesn't work.

A lot of British comedy cinema from the 1960s was powered by the apocryphal notion that we are an island of prigs, prudes and scaredy-cats when it comes to sex. Rubber-faced *Carry On...* stalwart Kenneth Williams built a cottage industry out of blanching in horror at anything his comically PC characters would perceive as undue naughtiness. Dominic Cooke's *On Chesil Beach*, adapted from a dour novella by Ian McEwan, transforms cultural myth into hard fact, framing the marriage bed not as a venue for bawdy larks, but face-clawing anguish.

It's 1962 and Florence (Saoirse Ronan) and Edward (Billy Howle) are about to get hitched prior to honeymooning at the scenic shingle bank of the title. By rights, the pair should be extremely loved up and excited for the years of lustful frolicking that lay ahead of them. In reality, it's like they've both signed a two-way death pact and they're working out who's going to chug the poison first. Even though this is a story about youthful innocence tainted by biological necessity, it is also one which may be tough for modern viewers to comprehend. Sex is framed as a violent invasion of privacy, a disgusting mode of gender-aligned torment and a vile dance learned through draconian medical pamphlets. Yet the film is not really interested in looking at physical action, as it is too busy admonishing a postwar generation too hung up on tradition to tell their kids what goes in where and why.

This is Cooke's directorial debut, though he arrives to film from a storied and successful career in theatre. During the film's initial stages, with its bright and plush establishing sequences buoyed by much admirably detailed production design, the switch from stage to screen is all but unnoticeable. Yet by the film's protracted, cosmically overwrought climax, you can almost see the footlights as the actors do their thing. The story is mostly told in flashback, detailing how the happy couple reached this juncture of high anxiety. The story goes out of its way to emphasise the star-crossed nature of the pairing, and how Edward and Florence through their interests and progressive worldview appear almost made for one another. He is brought up in a tumbledown cottage with a mother (Anne-Marie Duff) suffering from a mental impairment. Her blood runs blue, with parents who still see marriage an opportunity to expand and conquer. And we all know that a love which defies parental consent is the greatest love of all.

Even though the source material was written by a man, it's fascinating to consider how the story might have played had there been a woman behind the tiller. As is, there's a clear imbalance of empathy towards the worldly but ultimately chivalrous male character at the expense of his more timorous, sensitive female foil. The question at the centre of it all, however, is whether a bond of love can exist without physical consummation. And this conundrum is answered in rather abrupt fashion, even though the film appears to quickly undo its own thesis with a soppy, tacked on coda. It's a shame that the would-be lovers are morally unequal per this story's insidiously subjective telling, as Edward's torment is seen as more deserving of sympathy than Florence's.
DAVID JENKINS

Lek and the Dogs

Directed by
ANDREW KÖTTING
Starring
XAVIER TCHILI
Released
8 JUNE

ANTICIPATION.
Kötting is a very unpredictable director.

ENJOYMENT.
It's a tough but highly absorbing watch.

IN RETROSPECT.
Lek's story is a haunting one.

Lek and the Dogs opens on a desolate landscape, completely empty except for the naked figure we see scrambling across the ground on all fours. Is he man or beast? At this point in Lek's life, he doesn't seem to fit comfortably in either world.

This new film by British maverick Andrew Kötting is a loose adaptation of the acclaimed play 'Ivan and the Dogs' by Hattie Naylor, which was inspired by the true story of Ivan Mishukov. In 1996, four-year-old Ivan walked out of his family home in Moscow, away from the clutches of his mother's drunken and abusive boyfriend. He would live on the streets for the next two years, befriending a pack of wild dogs with whom he could scavenge and sleep. These animals offered him a greater sense of companionship and protection than he had ever experienced with his family, and he would flee with them whenever the police attempted to bring him back to the human world.

Ivan eventually did return to human life, re-learning speech and going on to live a relatively ordinary life, but the protagonist of Kötting's film has chosen to resume his existence with his canine friends, finding people too much to bear. "Safety is under the surface," Lek decides, before sharing his story from his dark subterranean den, muttering into a tape recorder with his bald head looming out of the shadows like Marlon Brando's Kurtz. Lek is played by Xavier Tchili, the French performance artist who previously appeared as characters with the same name in Kötting's *This Filthy Earth* and *Ivul*, and these films now feel like a loose thematic trilogy about society, family and our relationship with the

landscape. Andrew Kötting is a difficult artist to pin down, working prolifically and eclectically across a variety of media, but *Lek and the Dogs* feels like one of his most accomplished and fully realised works.

It's a remarkable audio-visual experience. While Lek's soliloquy gives the film its spine, Kötting layers multiple voiceovers on to the soundtrack; a body psychotherapist and a child psychologist give us an insight into the behaviour and emotional makeup of men and dogs, while a recording of Lek's wife – who he abandoned when she refused to join him underground – shades in his brief and unsuccessful attempt to re-enter society. Kötting's regular cinematographer Nick Gordon Smith evokes Tarkovsky's *Stalker* with his stark images of Lek wandering through the wastelands, but it's the director's imaginative use of archive footage that really impresses, as he skilfully uses it to illustrate Lek's experiences and to create a vivid portrait of the broken society he emerged from.

Lek and the Dogs is a dense and challenging film, but it's also a rewarding one that carries a powerful emotional charge thanks to Tchili's spellbinding lead performance. The film is about the legacy of childhood trauma, and how it can scar and warp an entire life, and as played by Tchili, Lek appears to be a genuinely tormented soul; it's as if each memory he retrieves for us is causing him physical pain. By the end of the film we understand why Lek has chosen to live this way, rejecting his own species and finding solace with another. "My dogs have never left me," he weeps, "but humans... they never hear."
PHIL CONCANNON

Monday Madness
£6* cinema tickets
every week

barbican

Curated seasons
New releases
Screen talks

barbican.org.uk/cinema

* Excludes 60p booking fee

CITY OF LONDON

The City of London
Corporation is the founder
and principal funder
of the Barbican Centre

Ismael's Ghosts

Directed by
ARNAUD DESPLECHIN
Starring
MATHIEU AMALRIC
MARION COTILLARD
CHARLOTTE GAINSBOURG
Released
1 JUNE

ANTICIPATION.
Early word from the Cannes premiere wasn't great.

ENJOYMENT.
To nobody's surprise, Desplechin keeps a lot of plates spinning effortlessly.

IN RETROSPECT.
Where most contemporary films could stand to lose an hour, Desplechin's latest could use an extra one.

No one who's ever encountered the work of Arnaud Desplechin will be surprised by the writer-director's habit of mashing together bits and pieces of repurposed and retrofitted story material. *Ismael's Ghosts*, his tenth film, not including two documentaries, since 1991, is energised by the depthless well of impatient beauty that fans of 2004's *Kings & Queen* and 2008's *A Christmas Tale* know well. Will Desplechin ever make another unprecedented masterpiece like his idiosyncratic period drama, *Esther Kahn*? Maybe not, but the dividends paid by his "Mathieu Amalric plays an addled yet high-octane creative, unable to cope with challenges monumental and mundane alike" mode are more than satisfactory.

The first hour of *Ismael's Ghosts* is dominated in large part by the story of alcoholic/insomniac/pill-popping filmmaker Ismael Vuillard (also the name of the musician Amalric played in *Kings & Queen*), more or less content in a long-term relationship with Sylvia (Charlotte Gainsbourg), until he's thrown off the rails by the return of his long-lost wife, Carlotta (Marion Cotillard). Intimations of the macabre hover about the place, in one moment recalling some off-kilter Ian McEwan tale, in the next, the gothic edge of an Ingmar Bergman seaside melodrama.

Phantoms that produce unendurable anxieties for the film's characters are exactly what Desplechin uses as a means to hitch one narrative wagon to the next. Ismael has maintained a lasting friendship with the father of his presumed-dead wife, celebrated film director Henri Bloom (László Szabó, in a role that once would have been occupied by the late Desplechin stock player Jean-Paul Roussillon). Bloom has been so

ensconced in a single, familiar rut of inconsolability that, when he's beset by the reality of his daughter's return, has nowhere to turn to but abject grief and psychotic denial. On the flip side, Carlotta struggles to cope with the fact that, while her father lives, the two are irreparably estranged, as if seeing each other on the far side of a dream. Ismael's espionage screenplay, based on the imagined life of his foreign-service brother (Louis Garrel), provides still another prime mover for this slippery film. Crafting hilariously incoherent John le Carré/*Homeland* boilerplate, Ismael turns his real and undoubtedly more grounded brother into a quicksilver imp of diplomatic legend, a jittery savant, a projection of his own permanent live-wire state into a world he can only imagine in a binge of drunk creativity, never fewer than three whiskeys deep at his laptop, his ashtray full.

Camerawork and cutting – even the occasional deployment of brazenly expressionist lighting effects – tell the tale of Desplechin's own impatience (coupled with the implicit trust he has in the audience's ability to keep up), flitting through story setups and double-backs with a weaving, staccato rhythm. A typical Desplechin feint occurs when he stops to burrow into a detail, a memory or a photograph, the pace of the film seeming to flag only in the manner of bated breath – a look before a leap. We're carried along by the exhilarating sensation of a storyteller eternally besieged by his own restlessness, but served in equal measure by an uncanny self-assurance. That *Ismael's Ghosts* seems to exist simultaneously on all its conflicting planes may be an illusion, but it is a stubbornly persistent one. **JAIME N CHRISTLEY**

Arnaud Desplechin

The director of *Ismael's Ghosts* describes how he forges a mask for each new movie.

The erudite French filmmaker explains his personalised working method, how he comes up with film titles and his new work, *Ismael's Ghosts*, about a scatty film director named Ismael (Mathieu Amalric) who is visited by a ghost from his past.

LWLies: In the film, Ishmael refers to himself as a "*fabricant de film*", which is like a manufacturer of film. Is that how you see yourself as a director? Desplechin: Yeah that's my word to describe my job.

Why do you use that term? You know what I love? The fact that he is saying I am a manufacturer, I knew that I had to make a portrait of an artist. My way to sort it out is to stay humble. I have problems with artists in film. They can be pretentious and have all these demons in their soul. It can be exasperating. So my way to sort this out is to have a humble artist. So, he's saying I'm just a manufacturer. Even if he is taking his job very seriously. I can't see myself as a filmmaker. I'm not a filmmaker. Who can say that? Maybe I am a

cinematographer? What am I doing for my living? I'm manufacturing a film. Writing is a thing I'm doing with my hands.

Are other people are allowed to call you a director? Yes, but I'm not allowed to.

As a director, Ismael, seems to hark back to a kind of the classic era of cinema in that he sleeps with his actresses, he has a gun and he walks away from the production. Is the character inspired by any real life people? I guess that Ismael is close to Mathieu [Amalric]. But he's not inspired by anyone real. I know Mathieu as a director and Mathieu isn't mad at all, he's quite reasonable. He's a wonderful, tremendous director, but not wild at all. Ismael embodies everything that we don't allow ourselves to do. To be clear, I have no gun. I'm terrified of guns. And I would never leave a set. It' not possible for me. Ismael doesn't give a fuck about anything. He's wild and that's why it was funny to depict the character – he overdoes everything.

The film explores the idea of a character who makes a decision to stop living their life at a certain point, and move in a new direction. Is that something you believe is possible? You always do a film to against the previous one. In *My Golden Days* [Desplechin's previous film] it was about the first experience, first love, the beginning, they were absolute beginners. This time I loved the fact that all the characters are not kids any longer. They have a second chance. I love this idea of having a second chance which is a pure American theme. Ismael is on the phone and

he is saying to Sylvia, I have to reinvent myself. And I believe that if you work hard on it, you can reinvent yourself.

What are your thoughts on the idea of director's cuts? Have you got any films that you've made that you'd want to go back to and tinker? With each film, I hope to find a mask and I can disguise myself and you won't recognise me. Each time I finish the film and the critics come to me and say, 'I recognise you' and I think, 'oh I've failed'. Then I have to make a new film, find a new mask and to try to invent myself again.

At what point in the process does the title come? Initially a film is not a film – it's a project, it's a flag to say, okay that's where we will go. So I put a flag on the hill and said that's where we're going. At first, I had a file on my computer and it was called "Escape" because I know that the guy was escaping to reinvent the woman in the attic. So it was called "Escape" and then the character of Carlotta appeared in the script and I said, 'I have to move my flag'. So there was another title which is "From the Dead" which is the French title of Hitchcock's *Vertigo*. The novella of 'D'entre les morts' that was adapted for *Vertigo*, but I thought, 'yeah this one is too close to *Vertigo*' and then came *Ismael's Ghosts*. Plural, so several ghosts All these ghosts which are surrounding him, and he is trying to escape from them. He also has to find Sylvia's brother who is a ghost too – a nice ghost. When she is mentioning it, you think, 'Okay, it's just a detail in dialogue.' And when he reappears at the end of the movie, it's like, 'oh fuck he was real, he did exist!' That's Sylvia's ghost. So each one of them has to deal with his or her ghosts. ◉

Mary Shelley

Directed by
HAIFAA AL-MANSOUR
Starring
ELLE FANNING
MAISIE WILLIAMS
DOUGLAS BOOTH
Released
6 JULY

ANTICIPATION.
Haifaa Al-Mansour's follow-up to Wadjda*!!*

ENJOYMENT.
Haifaa Al-Mansour's follow-up to Wadjda*??*

IN RETROSPECT.
A confused and confusing beast.

The story of Mary Shelley (née Mary Wollstonecraft Godwin) is ripe for the biopic treatment, containing as it does young love, romantic poets, disgrace, tragedy and events leading up to the creation of the almighty horror parable, 'Frankenstein' subtitled 'or, The Modern Prometheus'. All of this took place in England of the early 1880s while Shelley was still a teenager. On paper, who better to bring this intense female struggle to life than Haifaa Al-Mansour, the Saudi Arabian director whose 2012 feature debut, *Wadjda*, is so vivid with the spirit of its plucky child subject.

There is entertainment to be derived from Mary Shelley, but perhaps not for the right reasons. Elle Fanning's central performance adds needed weight, but all around her the tone is bizarre and the performances hammy. Mary, her lover Percy Bysshe Shelley (Douglas Booth) and her stepsister, Claire Clairmont (Bel Powley), louche about drinking with Lord Byron (Tom Sturridge) at his manor. After they pull up in carriages, Byron flings open his front door, snarls, "Shelley", and comes striding over. The new arrivals freeze. But the anger was a put on, and on reaching the group Byron dramatically kisses Percy on the mouth. Flourishes like this abound. Everyone is something of a rake.

The story is so juicy that the film works in spite of itself, although the plinky-plonk three-note piano refrain that accompanies every scene becomes its own joke. Al-Mansour and her screenwriting partner, Emma Jensen, pump the dialogue full of swoons, especially in the opening stretch in which a 16-year-old Mary is wooed by the 21-year-old author Percy, who sends drippy love notes, and inspires murmuring about the "curdling of the blood and the quickening of the heart."

A motif of Mary's character is that she is defiantly interested in pursuing true feeling and does not mind if it costs her her reputation. "I fear nothing except that your meaningless words will scare me away from my desires," she snaps at her disapproving stepmother, shortly before her father, scandalised by her union with the married Bysshe-Shelley, kicks them both out. A female character as independent as she is creative as she is soulful is tantalising. Fanning's self-possessed turn makes her a force to admire, as she squares up to men who would use her body, demean her mind or deny her soul.

Mary Shelley ends up being an opportunity to enjoy Fanning's quality English accent. She is unquestionably the star of every scene – half-present to her companions and half looking inward at the monstrous feelings that will eventually become 'Frankenstein'. Her pensive watchfulness also doubles as a baffled commentary on the other performances. Bel Powley (wonderful in *The Diary of a Teenage Girl*) is over-styled, while Douglas Booth is at least 75 per cent pout. The film is gratifyingly on point with its gender politics and styled to perfection, with Caroline Koener's costumes offering a carousel of visual pleasures. But unlike Shelley's famous monster, the disparate parts Al-Mansour has assembled here do not move as one.
SOPHIE MONKS KAUFMAN

Hereditary

Directed by
ARI ASTER
Starring
TONI COLLETTE
GABRIEL BYRNE
ALEX WOLFF
Released
15 JUNE

ANTICIPATION.
*Early reports from Sundance
are promising.*

ENJOYMENT.
Welcome back, Toni Collette!

IN RETROSPECT.
*This is serious, glorious,
edge-of-your-seat horror.*

To quote the immortal words of Philip Larkin: "They fuck you up, your mum and dad. They may not mean to, but they do." This poetic indictment of familial relationships is brought to mind by Ari Aster's searing cinematic debut, *Hereditary*, in which the members of a middle-class, ostensibly normal family come to terms with the death of a relative and face the strange days that follow her funeral.

This unfortunate clan are the Grahams, consisting of artist Annie (Toni Collette), her husband Steve (Gabriel Byrne) and their two children, Peter (Alex Wolff) and Charlie (Milly Shapiro). Annie works as a miniaturist. She creates exquisite small-scale renderings of real-life scenarios which provide a crucial anchor to the story: as she contends with an impending gallery deadline as well as her mother's passing, it becomes clear that – as in her work – the devil is in the detail.

And what details there are to behold in the performances, chiefly from Collette as the frantic, fractured woman battling internal demons and the very real possibility of external ones too. She's gamely joined by Byrne, who gives a subtle, stern performance as her increasingly exasperated husband Steve, and impressive young'uns Alex Wolff and Milly Shapiro who hold their own as the Graham siblings. Wolff in particular has a striking vulnerability about him – rather than playing up a teenage archetype, he's wide-eyed and terrified; a messy, shrieking, infinitely relatable adolescent loser.

The film's intricate construction is complemented by Colin Stetson's unsettling Gaslini-adjacent score, and a rich, heavily-saturated colour palette that works in stark contrast with the progressively more eerie action that plays out against the small-town sunshine. In the age of the obligatory jump scare there are grizzly scenes aplenty, but Aster prefers a painful sense of impending dread which begins with the opening shot and refuses to rescind its grip until the final credits. It's possible to identify subtle cinematic nods to the likes of *Don't Look Now* and *The Shining* – notably in Shapiro's unnerving portrayal of a creepy kid at odds with the rest of her family (complete with an orange hoodie as unexpectedly haunting as Christine Baxter's red mac). Pawel Pogorzelski's crisp, ethereal cinematography seems influenced by John Alcott's iconic work with Kubrick. Rather than a derivative exercise in genre scalping, there's something fresh about the masterful way in which Aster examines the insidious nature of suburban inertia while playing on the very real fear of what we inherit from our parents, and in turn, what we pass onto future generations, wilfully or not.

Part relationship psychodrama, part ghost story, part exploration of inherited madness, *Hereditary* is a film which refuses to parlay into a set definition of horror, which is its twisting, slippery strength. It begs to be rewatched, reconsumed and resurrected so that some part of its spiralling weirdness might become more familiar. Although there's plenty of unsettling imagery present that's liable to haunt audiences for years to come, it's Aster's thematic ambition which transforms it into a smiling, intoxicating villain of a film that gets under your skin and sinks into the marrow of your bones. **HANNAH WOODHEAD**

Interview by **HANNAH WOODHEAD**

Illustration by **SOPHIE MO**

Toni Collette

The star of Ari Aster's wicked debut *Hereditary* talks grief, audiobooks, and why we should all go to the cinema more often.

Having first achieved cult reverence for her role as the awkward eponymous character in *Muriel's Wedding*, Toni Collette has worked as a chameleonic character actor for 25 years and counting. She delivers a blistering performance as Annie Graham in the terrifying metaphysical ghost story, *Hereditary* (reviewed page 77). When she called from the LA set of her next feature (Dan Gilroy's *Velvet Buzzsaw*), the Australian couldn't have been less like her on-screen persona – but was only too happy to talk us through the process of making a modern horror classic.

LWLies: What was your first response when you received the script for *Hereditary*? Colette: I really wasn't looking to do anything like that, which my agent knew, and they sent it to me saying "We really think you should check it out" – and they were right! I think the horror derives from the fact that before that kicks in, you actually really get to be with these people who are in quite a lot of pain – it's more a study on grief and family dynamics. When I read it, it felt heavy but in a really beautiful, honest way. It took its time, and it doesn't become ridiculous. The horror is an extension of what's happening – which is what makes it even scarier.

It's such a slow burn. You really see the way this whole family unravel. People have been quick to just categorise it as a horror film, but I think it's about so much more than jump scares or gore. And none of that is gratuitous. It's all down to Ari (Aster). I'm telling you, this guy is the real deal. I really didn't want to do anything heavy or emotional, but I just couldn't help myself because it was just so brilliant. When I met him he was so aware of what he wanted to do, and I realised I'd never worked with a director who was that thorough, and meticulous. It was an intense experience but it was very satisfying as well.

Do you see any similarities between Annie and the roles you've played in the past or did this feel like something completely different? Every character I've played feels different, but with Annie in particular, it was really nice to play someone where I wasn't afraid of her being unlikable. There's quite a narcissistic edge to her – she's so absorbed in her own pain and her own neurosis – but also a sense she needs to be taken care of, and that she's a little unhinged and vulnerable. Grief is hideous for people to go through; it's a part of life that's really difficult but it's taboo to talk about it. I love that the film tackles that, and the family all engage in it in a completely different way.

How do you find the necessary emotional space to perform these sorts of roles, which must be quite draining? I knew what was required of me

with *Hereditary*, and I could feel it somewhere inside of me, but it was a case of kind of holding everything at bay and resisting going there until it was absolutely necessary. Otherwise it would just be too much. It's not like I'm getting caught up in the story and suddenly feel like I'm the character – I think that's utter bullshit when actors talk like that. This role was a lot though, so I saved it for when the camera was rolling. I even tried not to think about it. It was just erupting when necessary.

I read an interview with you from 2002 where you said that "acting is a weird form of torture". Does that apply even more so to a film like *Hereditary*? When I first started acting I used to feel very overwhelmed by my emotions, and acting gave me an outlet to express myself. When I said that, I was probably trying to retain my own emotions, but my relationship with acting has changed over and over as I get older. I don't know how to do it other than give 100% so it does get a bit exhausting, but other than that, it's so exciting to work on something that feels special, which *Hereditary* did.

That sense of this being something special came across when I saw it. Everyone in the cinema seemed completely blindsided by it. I haven't seen it with an audience yet. I do like the fact also that this film in particular lends itself to the idea of watching it in a theatre, in a communal space and not just on your bloody phone or in bed. It's actually exciting to watch it with other people because you almost need that comfort. I don't want to get political, but I think that there's this push to make people live in a kind of ostracised, isolated way, and everything in society feeds that idea. I think the more people can come together the better.

What do you think it about the relationship between parents and children that makes it such a prime theme for horror films to explore? I think it's just really interesting to explore on every level and in every art form. The psychology of the connection between a parent and child is just so incredible. I'm listening to an audiobook called 'Difficult Mothers' at the moment – I wish I'd had it when I was shooting *Hereditary* because it is pretty much all about what we absorb from our prime caregiver. Certainly with Annie, her whole life she's just had an unsettled feeling and never understood it. One of the most horrible things about this movie is that there is no hope. No light and no hope. I think that's why people have had such strong reactions. And like you said – this isn't just a horror film. In essence, it's a family drama. People who just love horror will love this, but people who are interested in psychology, or who are interested in aesthetics, will be drawn to it too ◉

The Happy Prince

Directed by
RUPERT EVERETT
Starring
RUPERT EVERETT
COLIN FIRTH
EMILY WATSON
Released
1 JUNE

ANTICIPATION.
Who isn't wild about Wilde?!

ENJOYMENT.
*Wilde went through a lot
in his final years so it's
poetic justice that this
biopic put us through a lot.*

IN RETROSPECT.
*A poignant story that is almost
eclipsed by the egoistic frolics of
its creator.*

Everything you need to know about Rupert Everett's tonally baffling yarn about the final years of Oscar Wilde is contained in this fact: he could have made it nine years ago with Philip Seymour Hoffman in the lead, but he said no. Fast forward to the present day and, to the satisfaction of the screenwriter (Everett), the role of Wilde is played by Everett. Having a pop at directing for the first time is Everett. This trio of names accurately represents what unfolds in front of the camera. Rupert James Hector Everett has a gleeful time hamming up a caricature of the Britain's most enduring wit. Meanwhile the supporting cast battles to register performances of a more naturalistic pitch, spanning stoical (Edwin Thomas as the loyal Robbie Ross) to catty (Colin Morgan as good-time babe Bosie) to tremulous (Emily Watson scandalously frittered as Wilde's ailing and estranged wife Constance).

The setting is Paris, 1897 to '90. Wilde is living incognito under the pen name 'Sebastian Melmoth' after jail time for "sodomy and gross indecency" – in other words, for daring to be an out, gay man in Victorian society. Green around the gills and soulsick, he no longer survives on writing income but on aid from loyal friends. Readings from his 1888 children's story, *The Happy Prince*, (published when Wilde was the toast of London) provide a frame and the film camps out in its ethos of finding content within humility. Marinated in Wilde's sublime words, the down 'n' out in Paris situation has a gutter-poetry type of dignity, replete with the usual bohemian trappings: absinthe, elegant speeches and a much younger, paid-for boy.

Wilde liked to "live in the atmosphere of love" and sensual consolations take the place of the real deal until a blast from the past arrives by train. Enter Lord Alfred Douglas aka Bosie aka the lover with whom Wilde enjoyed the public liaison that led to his incarceration. Bosie is all sharply-planed cheekbones and family money. To the despair of friends who want Wilde to behave discreetly, but to the pleasure of audiences who enjoy scantily-clad male frolics, the pair embark on a hedonistic European sortie.

Someone who scans as the love of your life when life is charmed can take on a more conditional quality after a fall. Wilde is soon back in Paris lodgings, the worse for wear. If *only* Everett had trusted his dark material and not seen fit to 'jazz' it up with zany camera flourishes and a jarringly loud and syrupy score. Quotes from Wilde's original works are shoehorned into every available gap, highlighting how far the independent efforts of The Everett Show fall from those of his muse.

Nonetheless, there is a perverse charm to watching what is so clearly a passion project driven by a creator's sincere desire to celebrate a personal hero. While the experience of watching this chaotic and tonally incoherent biopic could not be recommended on the grounds of art, there is a more persuasive case to be made on the grounds of curiosity, for it is proof positive of the famous opening line from The Ballad of Reading Gaol: "Each man kills the thing he loves."
SOPHIE MONKS KAUFMAN

The Breadwinner

Directed by
NORA TWOMEY
Starring
SAARA CHAUDRY
SOMA CHHAYA
NOORIN GULAMGAUS
Released
25 MAY

ANTICIPATION.
Very keen to see what Ireland's Cartoon Saloon comes up with next.

ENJOYMENT.
A moving tale of a young woman taking desperate measures to sock it to the Taliban.

IN RETROSPECT.
A fiery takedown of fundamentalism, bigotry and oppression of all stripes.

With films like *The Secret of Kells* and *Song of the Sea* on their production roster, it was clear that Ireland's Cartoon Saloon were an animation house on the make. Nora Twomey's heartbreaking *The Breadwinner* seals their status as a word class player in the field of thoughtful, poetic and idiosyncratic feature animation. Their mode is social realism tinged with folkloric fantasy, though this film dials back the faeries and magic and drops us in the politically unstable hellhole of Kabul, Afghanistan circa 2001. It follows a family scraping together a meagre living in which every grain of rice and every raisin are essential for survival. Doltish Taliban enforcers swagger around the streets and impose their tyrannical rule, which is bad news for everyone, but especially the women.

The film's title refers to Parvana, the family's tenacious middle daughter who concocts a crafty scheme of resistance when their father is jailed on a trumped up charge. With the man of the house out of the frame, and women banned from wandering the streets without a male chaperone, even to purchase food, it appears as if a death sentence has been passed by proxy. But Parvana has a plan that is so seditious it verges on the unthinkable – just what she needs to get around the arrogant men in charge. More than a pitched battle of enlightenment versus ignorance, Twomey's film chips away at the absurdity of religious extremism while making a plea for a society which updates its laws in line with natural cultural evolution. It also suggests that the tighter the stranglehold of power, the more prone the people are to embrace subversion to ensure their freedom.

The atrocities of 9/11 aren't mentioned, even though the early rumblings of conflict are teased throughout. These characters have little interest in the world beyond their local border – and for good reason. *The Breadwinner* doesn't depict the Afghan people as victims of western aggression, even though that's where its story inevitably leads. The micro-scale civic victories take on an even more bittersweet hue when it becomes clear that everyone will be punished for the Taliban's crimes. Parvana dutifully reads a story to her toddler sister in which a boy faces his manifold fears to bring prosperity back to his village. Even though this tall tale offers a handy continuous commentary on the brutal realities, it also operates as a celebration of art as cosy refuge from life's torments.

The animation style is bold, crisp and unshowy, and serves the modest desert-village setting nicely. The film avoids wacky humour and demographic-targeting stereotypes, but never feels too po-faced or downbeat as a result of that. It also offers a careful and unromantic depiction of Central Asia, working as a necessary corrective against works which exoticise the region and culture. The constant looping back to the story-within-the-story becomes a little tiresome after a while, especially in the film's dramatic final stretch where the reality is now more absurd than the fiction. Yet the blunt-force power of the film is undeniable, even as it climaxes on a note of hopeful resignation. And while its message of female empowerment is wrought from a highly specific time and context, it goes without saying that it has much to say about the treatment of women from all walks of life.
DAVID JENKINS

Edie

Directed by **SIMON HUNTER**
Starring **SHEILA HANCOCK, KEVIN GUTHRIE,**
PAUL BRANNIGAN
Released **25 MAY**

I n *Edie*, the veteran actor Sheila Hancock is on career-best form as a woman – also named Edie – scorned by a suffocating marriage of thirty years, desperate to make up for lost time. Her husband's death sends her on a quest for rediscovery that so happens to include scaling one of Scotland's most challenging mountains. Simon Hunter's latest feature (his first after 2008's sci-fi adventure *Mutant Chronicles*), which premiered to standing ovations at last year's Edinburgh International Film Festival, is inspiring and attractively shot to make full use of its setting. The rocky terrain reflects the hardships life has thrown at Edie, while the beauty signalling hope and optimism for the future. It has the makings of a welcome-to-Scotland advert at times, but Hancock always steers the film back on track. Edie's life up until now has been consumed by her husband and his illness. But now, at the age of 84, she's packed her bags and hightailed it to the highlands with a steely determination pushing her along even when it all seems like too much.

There's a scene midway through the film where she ventures off alone, only to be trapped in a rainstorm, fumbling with the mechanics of her tent. It's admittedly distressing. Her own drive, however, persists and is aided by Johnny (Kevin Guthrie), a local mountaineering shop owner whose initial scepticism of Edie's abilities thaw, leading to a wonderful oddball relationship between the two that awards the film a lovely comic touch. He's not so much her saviour, more a true friend and keen supporter. Elizabeth O'Halloran's script works best as a character study, but falls short elsewhere, putting more responsibility on Hancock's shoulders. But, true to her talent, she handles this with poise and wit. And for that, plus the undeniably empowering message of a woman reclaiming her life at its core, *Edie* is worth the time and investment. **JAMIE NEISH**

The Secret of Marrowbone

Directed by **SERGIO G SÁNCHEZ**
Starring **GEORGE MACKAY, ANYA TAYLOR-JOY,**
CHARLIE HEATON
Released **13 JULY**

S omeone could make a lot of money by inventing a system which helps homeowners feel safe visiting their attic space. A dusty, dimly-lit attic plays a key role in this dramatically underpowered mid-century chiller, in which the eccentric Marrowbone family are forced to deal with both the literal and metaphorical demons who have chosen to reside above their heads. George MacKay is Jack, the oldest of four siblings charged with laying low in a spacious, chicly distressed American farmhouse following the death of their mother. Once Jack hits 21, he can lay claim to the property and live there legally. Yet there are problems, such as a nosey local lawyer (Kyle Soller), and the arrival of a man who may be their estranged father and the reason why they fled overseas from England. Their only friend is personable librarian Allie (Anya Taylor-Joy), who also lives a solitary life despite being warm for Jack's form.

Writer/director Sergio Sánchez takes a fair old time to introduce his intriguing players and sunny setting in the hope that he can later fire out a glut of gnarly plot twists. The problem with the film is that it is most interesting when doing as little as possible, such as watching the kids roam about the house, picking summer fruits or dashing through the surrounding woodland. The revelations, when they arrive, chip away at any credibility and emotion the film might have generated, making it feel like a mechanised boobytrap rather than an engaging and tragic exploration of the coping mechanisms we develop to deal with trauma. The actors appear to be going through the motions in order to serve an increasingly silly storyline which outstays its welcome by a good half-an-hour. It all just about comes together in the end, but it's strange that a film which tries so hard to be surprising can be so predictable. **DAVID JENKINS**

ANTICIPATION. *A film about an 84-year-old woman climbing a mountain in Scotland?* **3**

ENJOYMENT. *An inspiring resilience test with a career-best turn from Sheila Hancock.* **4**

IN RETROSPECT. *An uplifting character study that's definitely worth a look.* **4**

ANTICIPATION. *A hot young cast run about an old haunted house. Could be worse?* **3**

ENJOYMENT. *And, it transpires, it could be so, so much better.* **2**

IN RETROSPECT. *A retro chiller with positively no new or interesting moves.* **2**

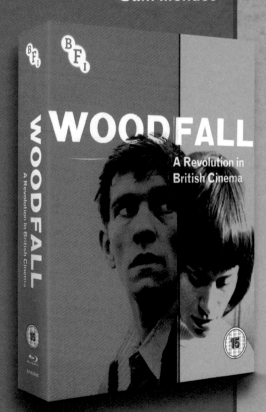

That Summer

Directed by **GÖRAN HUGO OLSSON**
Starring **PETER BEARD, LEE RADZIWILL,
EDITH BOUVIER BEALE**
Released **15 JUNE**

Swedish director Göran Hugo Olsson has formed a niche for himself out of editing found footage into documentary essays, kind of like adopting homeless children instead of adding another soul to the global population. "There is absolutely no need for a person like me to make a film," is his bracingly humble logic behind works such as *The Black Power Mixtape 1967-75* (2011), *Concerning Violence* (2014) and now *That Summer*. Softer in tone than the former titles, which engaged deeply with the fight against structural racism, his latest is also gentler than the celebrated Albert and David Maysles documentary, *Grey Gardens* (1975), which bears a comparison as this new/old film takes place in the same chaotic East Hampton's house.

Composed of four reels of gratifyingly grainy footage shot during the summer of 1972, this is an airy and full-hearted monument to the overshadowed ones. Lee Radziwill, sister of Jackie Bouvier/Kennedy/Onassis, is the hook who draws her filmmaker beau Peter Beard to the wild home of her relatives, Big and Little Edie, intending to make a story about her childhood. Focus shifts as she finds the mother and daughter recluses who shot to notoriety after Health Department raids on their dilapidated mansion were reported in the press. Lee, who is sidelined in the Maysles doc, is cast as a romantic figure wafting in and out of shot, warmly liaising with her cousins on the matter of home improvement, "She was so beautiful" says a present-day Peter Beard in voice-over. He is pretty romantic himself, shown on hands and knees making giant nostalgic artworks.

While the Maysles' documentary has a certain terseness, the optimistic sensibility of Peter Beard permeates this ambling slice of summer life, showing the Edies as somehow freed by their eccentric station in life, and almost childishly delighted by the presence of their cherished Lee. "Just be natural, that's the greatest beauty you can have," says Big Edie, eating ice-cream. She's not wrong. **SOPHIE MONKS KAUFMAN**

ANTICIPATION. *One doc and one HBO drama deep is time to ask: "Do we need more* Grey Gardens *content?"*

ENJOYMENT.
Captures the dreamy warmth of summer love.

IN RETROSPECT.
A tribute to the spirited ones.

Pin Cushion

Directed by **DEBORAH HAYWOOD**
Starring **LILY NEWMARK, JOANNA SCANLAN,
LORIS SCARPA**
Released **13 JULY**

Capricious teen Iona (Lily Newmark), and her smothering mother, Lyn (Joanna Scanlan), move to a small town for a fresh start in Deborah Haywood intriguing and moving debut feature, *Pin Cushion*. Both optimistically attempts to fit in to a community which does everything it can to repel them. Through the course of this vivid drama, the pair lose control and are driven apart, despite experiencing similar rejection.

The use of familiar coming-of-age tropes doesn't prevent the film from feeling fresh, as it boasts a unique aesthetic and twin plotlines following mother and daughter. The consequences of Iona's slut shaming are paralleled with Lyn's mental deterioration at the hands of various female bullies. Here, Haywood proves that this type cruelty thrives in the adult world as much as it does the adolescent. Most of the film is shot in close proximity to the characters, which emphasises their state of claustrophobia. The naivety of Haywood's protagonists leads to their manipulation, their differences are mocked and there is even some gothic retribution thrown in. Newmark mesmerises as Iona, performing her complex arc from innocence to apathy while leaving her essential purity in tact. Scanlan, meanwhile, is haunting as the hunchbacked Lyn and it's interesting to see the actor in a non-comic role that isn't comedic.

Haywood's eccentric style can be seen in every setting and costume, but this never distracts or feel out of place. Instead, it allows the moments in which she does over-indulge in it to feel like a natural extension of the characters' quirkiness; in one scene, sparkles cascade around a newly made-up Iona, in another a bathtub is filled with flowers. The score is simultaneously ethereal and eerie, just as the sweetness of these appearances can quickly turn sickly during the darker moments of the film. In all, a very fine first feature. **EVE JONES**

ANTICIPATION. *An indie director, a relatively unknown cast. Interest is piqued*

ENJOYMENT. *An interesting aesthetic and penetrating drama that develops meaning over its runtime.*

IN RETROSPECT. *A quiet and weird story, beautifully executed by Haywood.*

Arcadia

Directed by **PAUL WRIGHT**
Released **21 JUNE**

Filmworker

Directed by **TONY ZIERRA**
Starring **LEON VITALI, RYAN O'NEAL, DANNY LLOYD**
Released **18 MAY**

"I t is a country which for centuries has enjoyed a special fame, and there's nowhere like it on Earth!" Well, quite. These words, plucked from a tweedily patronising '50s documentary and placed squarely at the beginning of Paul Wright's fragmentary archive-footage odyssey through the changing relationship between Britons and their landscape, can't help but engender a mix of emotions in the native breast. Britain is certainly enjoying a sort of special and unwelcome fame at the moment, but how did it come to this? What part – if any – has the land played in turning this bulldog breed against itself? How did this cradle of civility, this bastion of eccentricity, become just another country? What hardened the wooden walls of England so? And why did Duncan's horses turn and eat themselves?

Arcadia journeys from a sleepy post-War Hobbiton of barley wine and hedgerows, through the beads, beards and bushes of '60s psychedelic folk revival and on to the glue-sniffing Mordor of Punk Britannia in search of clues. It discovers a distant land of kangaroo boxing, water diviners, Mighty Boosh-style thistle masks and a profusion of llamas, cheese rolling loonies, pentagrams and enormous chalk penises. A land where grievances are sorted out the old-fashioned way – with a free-for-all game of outlaw street rugby that descends into something approaching a riot. A land where charm, individuality and community shine through. Would that it were so...

Helped immeasurably by a lysergic soundtrack from Adrian Utley (Portishead) and Will Gregory (Goldfrapp), *Arcadia* layers its tumbling images to form a portrait of an idiosyncratic nation that hasn't so much lost its way, but rather fallen out of love with itself. The Sex Pistols told us that there was no future in England's dreaming, but looking back from where we stand now it doesn't look so bad. At least we were all in the same strange dream. **ADAM LEE DAVIES**

W hether it was making Tom Cruise do 95 takes of walking through the same door during the filming of *Eyes Wide Shut* or harshly bullying Shelley Duvall so she acted with the right level of fear in *The Shining*, director Stanley Kubrick's exhaustive methods for achieving cinematic perfection are well documented. *Filmworker*, a look at the life of Leon Vitali, who gave up a successful career in acting to become Kubrick's right hand man, achieves something fresh by showing what it was like to live under the rule of the dictatorial genius on a 24/7 basis. From the off, it's clear Vitali maintains a passionate, if slightly creepy, love for Kubrick. Sitting next to a Kubrick cuddly toy and describing his audition for *Barry Lyndon* (he ended up playing the crucial role of Lord Bullingdon), Vitali's lips quiver as he almost sensually describes how the director's handshake, "sent a buzz right through you."

Filmworker focuses on Vitali's vital contributions to Kubrick's filmography. He was responsible for casting young Danny Torrance (Danny Lloyd) and the murdered Grady twins in *The Shining* as well as helping R Lee Ermey "achieve perfection" as the drill sergeant in *Full Metal Jacket*. Yet director Tony Zierra's documentary is at its best when it questions the ethics behind how Kubrick consistently pushed Vitali to the edge. Vitali did everything from editing film trailers and scouting locations to setting up video monitors in every room of Kubrick's estate so the director could keep tabs on his sick cat Jessica. Sure, it sags at times and the editing is a little rough, but at its core *Filmworker* is a touching love letter to the obsessive process of filmmaking and the sacrifice we make to achieve something that's creatively unblemished. Throughout, Zierra makes it obvious he believes Kubrick was the true love of Vitali's life. However, by the time *Filmworker* reaches its conclusion, it seems like that feeling may have been mutual. **THOMAS HOBBS**

ANTICIPATION. *Any documentary culled from the archives of the BBC and BFI has got to be worth a look, no?*

ENJOYMENT. *As British as Arthur Scargill and Jim Davidson covered in marmalade and chased through Lord's.*

IN RETROSPECT. *Leave or remain,* Arcadia *is something you can point to as a prime example of why.*

ANTICIPATION. *Do we really need another Stanley Kubrick documentary?*

ENJOYMENT. *Offers up fascinating insight into the risks and rewards of a life behind the camera.*

IN RETROSPECT. *By revealing the darker side of Kubrick, we're given an original take on his legacy.*

Budd Boetticher

A plush new Blu-ray box set offers occasion to celebrate this horseriding, bullfighting artisan of the feature western.

Budd Boetticher worked in multiple genres – the gangster picture, the film noir thriller, the war movie – but his reputation rides high in the saddle on the back of his westerns. This is appropriate, for Boetticher's pared-down picturemaking style is close to the just-the-necessities ethos of the western. Working sometimes with 13-day shoots, he turned out unhurried films reflecting a serene confidence in what went where and why. His best westerns are films that travel light, conserve their energy and their resources, don't waste a word or gesture or a set-up. They aren't great because of evident ambition or mythic dimension, but because of their ability to distill, condense, encapsulate.

Boetticher's filmmaking cut to the bare essentials, and perhaps this is how he viewed his own life, though from the outside one sees merrily squandered opportunities. When he died in 2001 at age 85, he had been only sporadically employed as a director of fiction features in the years after 1960, when he interrupted his career to head to Mexico to pursue a passion project that swallowed up much of the decade ahead, a documentary on his old friend the bullfighter Carlos Arruza. His career never fully recovered from this abrupt abnegation, but what he'd done up to that point was enough to install him as the subject of a particularly enthusiastic mini-cult, some of who would pilgrimage through the years to pay homage to that rare bird Boetticher, one of the last surviving specimens of the old-school tough-guy director and brawling Hemingway-esque existentialist. Among those passing through was Taylor Hackford, making a PBS profile on Boetticher. Introducing a recent screening of *The Tall T* (1957) in New York, Hackford recalled shooting at the old man's ranch in Chatsworth, giving a graphic description of Boetticher, after staying on horseback at length to facilitate reshoots, dismounting and dropping trow to display his bleeding hemorrhoids and exploded anus, a souvenir of a rectal goring received in the bullfighting ring.

The man and his ass and his reckless rootin' tootin' life were plenty colourful enough to be remembered, but his work quietly speaks for itself. At the centre of Boetticher's legend are his films of the mid-to-late 1950s, a collection of which can be found on a new box set from the Indicator label, *Five Tall Tales: Budd Boetticher & Randolph Scott at Columbia*. The movies here belong to the so-called "Ranown Cycle," a series of six or possibly seven westerns starring Randolph Scott, mostly produced by Scott and Harry Joe Brown – from whence "Ranown" – and mostly written by Burt Kennedy, a pure poet of ranch lingo and western speechifyin'. (The liminal entry in this grouping is 1959's *Westbound*, directed for Warners to fulfill a contractual obligation, which features Scott but no other key personnel.)

Oscar "Budd" Boetticher had ridden a long way to make these terse, dry, sometimes gorgeous plein air movies. He was raised in an atmosphere of serene moneyed comfort, but distinguished himself with a knack for squeezing into tough and dirty spots, taking a precipitous tumble from Midwestern gentility to being a fortysomething gringo malingering in a south-of-the-border jail cell. After losing both of his parents early in life he was brought up in Evansville, Indiana by the head of a prosperous hardware concern. He loved football, was a standout at Ohio State University, but quit school demoralised after a knee injury decimated his professional prospects. Now adrift, on the first leg of a South American tour in Mexico City in 1939, Oscar fell in love with a new sport, bullfighting, and stayed on to study the art under such celebrated toreros as Don Lorenzo Garcia and Fermin Espinoza. This skill-set would eventually provide him his Hollywood break, teaching star Tyrone Power the ropes as "bullfighting advisor" on Rouben Mamoulian's *Blood and Sand* (1941).

Consulting on the cutting of an action scene in that movie with editor Barbara McLean, Boetticher discovered his life's third great passion in film work, and so he stuck around the movie town, and began to climb the ranks from the bottom rungs. He made his break into directing at the Columbia "B" unit run by Sam and Irving Briskin, and kept on the grind making cheapos at Poverty Row outfits including Eagle-Lion and Monogram Pictures. Some of the pictures he made in this period aren't without their pleasures – noir entries *Assigned to Danger* and *Behind Locked Doors* (both 1948) are standouts – but Boetticher felt himself floundering in the minor leagues, and sought to pull himself out by writing a screenplay of his own.

The resulting film, *Bullfighter and the Lady* (1951), made under the auspices of John Wayne's Batjac Productions, was what kicked Boetticher upstairs. Drawing not a little on Boetticher's personal history, the film stars Robert Stack as an American in Mexico who takes up bullfighting in order to win the heart of a local señorita. It was the movie on which Oscar Boetticher started to call himself Budd, and the only one for which Budd was Oscar nominated – he lost Best Story to *Seven Days to Noon* (1950). Its success led to a contract at Universal, and to the beginning of Budd's career as a director of principally westerns. But he was restless, at odds with Universal's house style from the get-go, and probably temperamentally unsuited to the life of an assembly-line contract director. As an independent he had rather more luck, as in the case of *The Killer is Loose* (1956), a baroque thriller strikingly shot by longtime Boetticher buddy Lucien Ballard, whose vengeance-driven plot anticipates the westerns to come.

It was with horse opera *Seven Men from Now* (1956), again for Batjac, that Boetticher began his greatest period of productivity – and the Ranown Cycle. The movie lays out the basic elements that will be arranged and rearranged throughout the Cycle movies. There's a taciturn protagonist, always played by an increasingly weatherbeaten Scott, who is bound to a hard and fast personal code. He lives by his terms, but is far from uncompromised by the violent world in which he lives: Scott plays soldiers-of-fortune and bounty hunters, and in *Decision at Sundown* (1957), his character is close to pathological, fixated on terminating smoothie John Carroll, the last – but far from only – man that his wife cuckolded him with before her suicide. Counterpoised to the Scott character you have a loquacious antagonist frequently in conversational close quarters with the protagonist, played in S*even Men* by a Cheshire grinning, lime green scarf-clad Lee Marvin, though Richard Boone, Pernell Roberts, Claude Akins, and Craig Stevens variously step into the part. There may be other proper villains at play, but this antagonist is no more fully bad than the Scott character fully good, and every bit as human in his charisma and clearly communicated motives.

In the middle of this masculine brinksmanship there is a woman, and behind her, usually, the unquiet memory of another woman. Scott's characters boast a plethora of dead wives and rankling, vengeful grudges against the men he blames for their deaths, the memory of matrimony stirred by the women he encounters along the trail: Gail Russell, Karen Steele, Virginia Mayo, Nancy Gates. Scott, born into the straight-backed comportment of a Virginia gentlemen, places himself in the role of the protector of threatened femininity, while his antagonists, more forthright in matters of sex, often razz our hero for his chivalric posturing and hypocrisy – Roberts in *Ride Lonesome* (1959) isn't above trying to deal himself in. In *Seven Men from Now* this results in one of the steamiest no-contact scenes in cinema, as Scott beds down beneath the covered wagon in which Russell is sleeping, the two talking to one another quietly, close but very far away. (*The Tall T* is unique in sending Scott away with a living woman, Maureen O'Sullivan.)

What are these Ranown movies about? Well, they're about 70-something minutes. Skirting their deep pools of ambivalence they open towards their characters, we can say they are, broadly, against needless cruelty and violence and against small-town potentates, like those who rule Agry Town in *Buchanan Rides Alone* (1958), and against the racial bias levelled against Manuel Rojas' character in that same film. But more than addressing any moral or social question, they're about capturing the tenor of conversations that take place while sipping a cup of coffee outside at night or a ripple of exchanged glances that tell the real story behind official bluster, about filming seemingly simple and straightforward scenes in such a way as to capture the complex, multivalent operations at work within any group of people pursuing their own individual motives. And they are about the pleasure of their own making, of doing and undoing and doing again. Perhaps the finest piece of criticism pertaining to these films is My Budd, a tribute painting by Manny Farber that shows a tabletop view of scattered ephemera pertaining to Ranown pictures – doll-like westerners, a toy train track, a scattering of rocks, a slab of sky blue – elements fixed on the canvas, though seemingly inviting play, re-arrangement.

This tribute may have sprung from some imagined affinity on Farber's part, for he had left behind criticism to teach and paint, just as Boetticher had gradually left cinema alone, contenting himself to raise his Andalusian horses. The last Ranown movie, *Comanche Station*, was released in 1960, also the year of Boetticher's *The Rise and Fall of Legs Diamond* (1960), which gives centre-stage to the antagonist figure in the form of Ray Danton's cold, preening gangster-gigolo. Then Boetticher was shortly off to pursue the White Whale of his Arruza movie, to return to a Hollywood where he was largely forgotten outside of a cache of admiring cineastes. He made Audie Murphy's last feature, *A Time for Dying* (1969), but even as work dried up, his influence didn't. His contemporary, Don Siegel, directed Boetticher's screenplay *Two Mules for Sister Sara* (1970) when nobody else in town was taking Budd's calls, and before Sam Peckinpah lit off on his own trail he produced the Scott-starring, Ballard-shot *Ride the High Country* (1962), a work heavily indebted to the Ranown films.

You can bemoan the movies that were lost because Boetticher decided to split for Mexico, though it might just as well be said that he wouldn't have been able to make the films that he did if he wasn't the sort of man to up and leave it all behind. It was this dedication to the physical life, the preoccupation that pulled him after Arruza, that allowed Boetticher to put flesh-and-blood onto western archetypes to a rare degree. This doesn't just apply to their vivid violence and the solid thunk of bodies in saddles, but to the degree to which they allow an entire cast of characters their individual agency. To borrow from Renoir, everyone in the Ranown movies has their reasons – and most of them have a gun to back them up ◉

Five Tall Tales: Budd Boetticher & Randolph Scott at Columbia, 1957-1960 is released by Arrow Films on 21 May.

UK DISTRIBUTION

Iron Monkey

Directed by **YUEN WOO-PING**	**1993**
Starring **RONGGUANG YU** **DONNIE YEN** **JEAN WANG**	*Released* **18 JUNE**
	Blu-ray

F ollowing the release of *The Matrix* in 1999, there was a surge of interest in the work of Hong Kong director and martial-arts choreographer Yuen Woo-ping. Perhaps his crowning glory is the 1993 epic *Iron Monkey*, a fictionalised adventure in the life of Chinese folk hero Yang Tianchun. A mild-mannered doctor by day, by night Yang robs from the rich to give to the poor as The Iron Monkey, a beloved avenger with far more stylistic flare than his western counterpart Robin Hood. When fellow martial arts expert/healthcare professional Wong Kei-ying rocks up in town with his young son Wong Fei-hung he becomes accidentally implicated in the Iron Monkey's antics, and Tianchun is forced to take a stand against the corrupt provincial governor once and for all.

Those familiar with Yuen's later work in *Crouching Tiger, Hidden Dragon* will recognise the ambitious, mesmerising action sequences that define *Iron Monkey*, particularly in the climactic confrontation scene which takes place high on bamboo poles above a treacherous fire pit. "Wire-fu" is its mainstay, combining the art of kung-fu with wire-work to create the exhilarating, supernatural high-kicks and flips which ensure the film slips into magical realist territory, providing it with the feel of a martial arts fairytale. While it's fair to say that the simplistic plot only really serves as a vehicle for these high-octane fight sequences, when they're as entertaining and exceptional as Yuen's, that's not necessarily a bad thing. In fact, intercut with slapstick comedy and exceptional shots of plush scenery, the fight scenes have more of an impact, and there's an earnest charm about Yuen's forthright depiction of gallant good guys and bumbling bad guys. His breathless 90-minute epic provides a fascinating insight in the Hong Kong movie scene at its early-'90s zenith. **HANNAH WOODHEAD**

Mishima: A Life in Four Chapters

Directed by **PAUL SCHRADER**	**1985**
Starring **KEN OGATA** **MASAYUKI SHIONOYA** **HIROSHI MIKAMI**	*Released* **11 JUNE**
	Blu-ray

T his is Paul Schrader's visually ravishing revision of what appears as a personal obsession with grown men prone to destroying themselves. As screenwriter of *Taxi Driver* and *Raging Bull*, and director of works such as *American Gigolo* and *Hardcore*, Schrader's early career is littered with male martyrs who fall victim to their own hubris, or who yearn for the world to turn backwards on its axis. His 1985 curveball *Mishima: A Life in Four Chapters* is an innovative and intuitive take on the traditional biopic which is entirely fitting of its idiosyncratic subject: the ultra-nationalist Japanese author, poet, actor, model and auto-didact, Yukio Mishima, who is brought to life with till-I-die commitment by the great Ken Ogata.

The film's present day depicts Mishima waking up and preparing for battle, assembling members of his private army, the Tatenokai, and heading towards the main headquarters of the Japanese self-defence forces with a view to staging a violent coup. Four flashbacks help to fill in the blanks, and are all inspired by personal or confessional elements in some of Mishima's most famous novels. The unreliable nature of these fictionalised memories is emphasised through the use of soundstage settings, neon lighting and large swathes of negative space. It's an amazing feat of distillation, somehow managing to pinpoint the key moments in Mishima's development as an artist and thinker without ever making it feel like it's trying to answer for his latter-day savagery. The final flashback is plucked from the 1969 novel 'Runaway Horses', and pre-stages, almost to the detail, our embittered subject's attempted overthrow. In this sequence, Schrader draws on the notion that the personal aspects of literature aren't always drawn from experience, but sometimes from projected desires. **DAVID JENKINS**

The Old Dark House

Directed by **JAMES WHALE**	**1932**
Starring **BORIS KARLOFF** **MELVYN DOUGLAS** **CHARLES LAUGHTON**	Released **21 MAY**
	Blu-ray

If you had to locate the cinematic ur-text of haunted house movies, James Whale's fruity bone-rattler from 1932, *The Old Dark House*, would likely be in contention. Enough time had passed for the conventions of the genre to be gently skewered, but the conceit was still ripe enough to be taken in a number of new and exciting directions. It begins as it should, on a rain-lashed evening in Wales. Three travellers are braving the road to Shrewsbury, but a landslide blocks their path and forces them to seek refuge in a sinister-looking country stack. After initially being turned away by catatonic and deformed butler, Morgan (Boris Karloff), they are invited in by Ernest Thesiger's wiry fusspot Horace Femm and his mad-eyed older sister, Rebecca (Eva Moore).

As the travellers merely attempt to survive through the night with whatever scant comforts available, it appears that their hosts are experiencing undue discomfort as a result of this nighttime imposition. The electric fails and the lights go out. Morgan hits the drink too hard. Locked doors and secret rooms are discovered. The Femm's macabre family saga is unfurled. Whale recreates the blustery Welsh countryside in an LA backlot with a fusty attention to detail. He goes easy on the pyrotechnics and jump scares, opting instead for an all-pervading sense of grotesque and perversity. In one sequence when Rebecca is delivering a mad monologue detailing her strict conservative worldview, the camera pulls away from her face and refracts the image through a warped mirror. The sudden effect is terrifying in and of itself, but also acts as a visual harbinger for things to come. This new restoration offers a vital reminder of the film's visual ingenuity and carefully calibrated atmospherics. **DAVID JENKINS**

Intimate Lighting

Directed by **IVAN PASSER**	**1965**
Starring **ZDENEK BEZUSEK** **KAREL BLAZEK** **MIROSLAV CVRK**	**OUT NOW**
	Blu-ray

People love making lists of their favourite movies. Sometimes we even narrow things down by specifying a genre or a goofy sub-category. Had more people seen Ivan Passer's sparkling 1965 feature debut, *Intimate Lighting*, one of the jewels of the so-called 'Czech New Wave', it would surely feature on more lists adjudicating the funniest films of all time. The set-up is simplicity defined: a concert cellist from Prague heads to the countryside with his wife to spend some time with an old pal, himself a violinist in a local orchestra. They hang out with the extended family, attend a funeral, sit down for a chicken dinner and stay up late nipping at the homemade brandy. There are no plot developments or dramatic events, Passer just captures the rough textures of family life.

City boy Peter (Zdenek Bezusek) is lightly bemused at the life he could've had, as his old pal Bambas (Karel Blazek) appears happy as a clam in his hand-built provincial castle. He and his family may lack refinement, but at no point does the film mock their daffy way of life. Passer's roving camera captures incidental detail, and he's a master of the deadpan reaction shot. Most of the jokes or bizarre proclamations are enhanced by the way the director always shows how they play to the room. There's an amazingly funny dinner sequence in which Bambas' beleaguered wife attempts to portion out a roast chicken so everyone gets a good bit, eventually courting the ire of her two young kids when she gives the legs to the guests. It's a film which flaunts its own louchness, to the point where it doesn't actually appear to be about anything more than a snapshot of domestic life in full, unapologetic flow. For anyone looking for a hearty giggle, this Blu-ray and a jug of extra thick eggnog is all you really need. **DAVID JENKINS**

Home
ENTS

I Vitelloni

Directed by **FEDERICO FELLINI**	**1953**
Starring **ALBERTO SORDI** **FRANCO FABRIZI** **FRANCO INTERLENGHI**	*Released* **28 MAY**
	Blu-ray

The desperate lengths that men go to keep it in their pants is an abiding trait in the cinematic oeuvre of Italian director Federico Fellini. His third feature, 1953's *I Vitelloni* (translation: The Bullocks), sees a gang of horned-up gadabouts pondering how they might escape the tedium of provincial life. There's the artist, the performer, the dreamer, the skirt-chaser (although would-be-rapist seems a more apt nomenclature) and the impressionable pretender. All discover that happiness is elusive, success is a mirage and the scales are always tipped against them ever falling out of line with their conservative Catholic upbringing. There isn't really a story to speak of – it's more like a spritzed-up soap opera in which the picturesque alleyways, quaint boutiques and tightly sanctioned pleasure-domes conspire to make the daily torpor feel ever more intense.

Fausto Moretti (Franco Fabrizi) has a habit of making the girls cry, humping and dumping as is his want. But not this time, as Sandra (Leonora Ruffo), voted "Miss Siren of 1953", is expecting, and a shotgun marriage is the only way that Fausto and his up-tight father can save face. He pervs around as best he can, often right under the nose of his doting, kindly spouse. It's like capture would be his only release, that being despised for his unchecked lust might actually get him chased out of this one horse town. Fellini loads up the film with rich colour and a real sense that he knows these people, he's lived with them, he's grown up with them, hell, he probably is one of them. Maybe it's sacrilege to say so, but Fellini was best when grounded in social realism rather than the insipid and shrill "intellectual" forays into the male psyche which cluttered the mid and later segments of his storied career. This is certainly one of his most fresh, vibrant and sincere works. **DAVID JENKINS**

Irma Vep

Directed by **OLIVIER ASSAYAS**	**1996**
Starring **MAGGIE CHEUNG** **JEAN-PIERRE LÉAUD** **NATHALIE RICHARD**	**OUT NOW**
	Blu-ray

There is something very timely about Olivier Assayas's coolly ironic feature *Irma Vep* in the way it captures a very specific cultural moment in the mid-'90s. Set in Paris, it chronicles the stalled and possibly ill-advised re-making of Louis Feuillade's classic silent-era serial, *Les Vampires*, which is seen by some as an act of vital homage, and others as high cinematic treason. It acts as a necessary callback to François Truffaut's under-the-hood exposé of the magic of moviemaking, *Day for Night*, from 1973, but with a more cynical and dejected edge. René Vidal is an ageing and emotionally volatile French auteur played by Jean-Pierre Léaud. His genius allows him a certain amount of wiggle room when it comes to his harried cast and crew.

In his attempt to bring *Les Vampires* to a generation fixated with Quentin Tarantino and John Woo (allied with his own erotic compulsions), he has cast Hong Kong martial arts star Maggie Cheung as the balletic cat burglar Irma Vep. She doesn't really know why she's been cast, but seeing this as a paying job and a potential way of cracking the west, she plays along, skipping between latex catsuit fittings, wine-soaked soirees and awkward cross-cultural clinches. Like so much of Assayas' best work, this is not a rounded drama which plays out in defined stages, more variations on a theme or a fictional essay piece. The chaotic production is seen through Cheung's eyes, and even though the director pulls no punches when it comes to depicting the tension between the commercial and artistic impulse, there's still romance underneath all the piles of paperwork. The film also boasts one of the great final scenes, a small reminder than even when an act of creation appears utterly futile, there's always a gem to be found among the wreckage. **DAVID JENKINS**

Jubilee

Directed by **DEREK JARMAN**	**1978**
Starring **JENNY RUNACRE** **NELL CAMPBELL** **TOYAH WILLCOX**	*Released* **18 JUNE**
	Blu-ray

When *Jubilee* was first released, fashion maverick Vivienne Westwood printed an open letter to Derek Jarman on a t-shirt, denouncing his film's representation (misrepresentation?) of punk as "the most boring and therefore disgusting thing I had ever seen". There are many adjectives one could use to describe Jarman's sophomore feature, but boring certainly isn't one of them. In this mind-boggling counter-culture odyssey, Queen Elizabeth I time-travels from her court to 1970s post-apocalyptic London, which is on the verge of collapse following the murder of the current monarch. Nefarious punk gangs roam the streets causing mischief and mayhem in a series of loosely-connected episodes, their exploits range from indulging in group sex to blasé murder, all set to an angry soundtrack including work by punk legends Chelsea, Siouxsie and the Banshees, Brian Eno, and Adam Ant.

Combining Shakespearean drama with nihilist havoc, it's a grizzly, spitting terror of a film, anchored by a fierce female fourtet who wreck havoc around the capital – in one memorable scene, they asphyxiate a male lover using red plastic sheeting and then dump his body in the Thames. Seeing women so clearly at the forefront of the carnage still holds a particular thrill – men are merely their playthings, used and discarded roughly when their purpose is served. At the film's end, the anarchists skip off to a pastoral idyll, lamenting "It's a tragedy that socialism and freedom weren't compatible". Lambasting the middle-class art school credentials of would-be punks, and predicting the commercialisation of punk that would soon follow his film's release, Jarman's grainy send-up of counter-culture is every bit as weird, bolshy and sneering as it was when it first ruffled punk mohawks back in 1978. **HANNAH WOODHEAD**

Ciao! Manhattan

Directed by **JOHN PALMER, DAVID WEISMAN**	**1972**
Starring **EDIE SEDGEWICK** **PAUL AMERICA** **WESLEY HAYES**	*Released* **18 JUNE**
	Blu-ray

For a film to be selected for review in this section, it's generally considered an act of tacit endorsement. The film might not be considered great, but certainly one that's worth seeking out. It's hard to know what to make of John Palmer and David Weisman's troubling 1972 feature *Ciao! Manhattan*, whether to see it as an squalid time capsule of elegant slumming and drug-addled rah-rahs or a tabloid snuff movie. Due to its association with Andy Warhol and his Factory set, the film is often referred to as an avant garde work, but that might just be another way of saying that it's both amateurish and incoherent, and accounting for stories of its troubled production, it's a cacophonous salvage job at best.

It is loosely billed as the life and times of a wild starlet named Susan Superstar who is played by impish Warhol protege, Edie Sedgewick (who is clearly not well). She is discovered at the beginning of the film in a state of high intoxication and semi undress, then subsequently lugged to a nearby mansion to dry out. Using audio interviews by the real Sedgewick, an impressionistic backstory is built up and it soon becomes obvious how she attained this state of thousand-yard semi-psychosis. Shortly after shooting wrapped, but before editing was completed, Sedgewick died of acute barbiturate intake and the film then duly became a case of art not so much imitating life, but anticipating it. The credits roll with a dedication to Sedgewick which seems more sleazy than earnest. Is it crass exploitation or just an example of the lassitude of screen biography and the idea of an actor giving a certain part of their true selves up for every performance? This new Blu-ray should help to answer those questions, but do approach this one with caution. **DAVID JENKINS**

First printing of
the newest, best
GIL BREWER
novel

AVON
25¢
830

THE
BITCH

Introducing byNWR.com...

Lost gems, newly polished

Those familiar with Little White Lies will know that we're fans of Nicholas Winding Refn – the Danish provocateur who's been subverting both genre and expectation since his 1996 debut feature, *Pusher*. Alongside his current Amazon-funded crime serial, Too Old to Die Young, he has another new project brewing. It's not a movie this time, but a scheme to bring movies made by other, lesser-known artists to a wider audience.

In his spare time, Refn is an avid collector of cinematic arcana. He owns a killer portfolio of exploitation movie posters, which were showcased in the gorgeous coffee table tome, 'The Art of Seeing'. His interest then evolved to the films themselves, and he became driven to salvage as many of these obscure and incendiary artworks as possible, scouring archives and private collections across the globe in search of celluloid manna.

His next step was to share all these treasures with a wider audience, and that's where byNWR comes in. Billed as a "cultural expressway" and a destination for movie lovers of all stripes, byNWR is a portal into Refn's personal movie archive, allowing patrons to see some of the weird and wonderful treasures that have influenced his work. To say that the films he has curated are rare would be something of an understatement. Many of them were in danger of being destroyed permanently or accidentally disposed of before he stepped in to save them from the trash pile. Refn's project is to bring these neglected works back to life, supercharging them all with brand new digital restorations.

This is a unique opportunity to catch up with films like Bert Williams's 1965 psychodrama *Nest of the Cuckoo Birds*, in which an escaped convict ends up taking refuge with an extremely strange family and which boasts one of coolest earworm theme songs in all of cinema. Or what about *Night Tide*, Curtis Harrington's psychedelic mermaid horror from 1961 in which a young Dennis Hopper falls for a young sea siren on the California coastline? You must catch JL Anderson's lost 1967 masterpiece *Spring Night, Summer Night*, a romantic and nonjudgmental portrait of family and poverty in Ohio's rural communities.

The deal is that every month a new film will appear on the site, and alongside it will be a cornucopia of stories, features, galleries, essays and general tall tales to offer vital background and context. First up to the plate was maverick biographer and Refn wingman Jimmy McDonaugh, and as of 1 June, Little White Lies are going to be presenting three of the films, starting with *Night Tide* . There is a catch, and that is everything on the site is completely free. So head on down to byNWR.com and make a discovery of your own.

byNWR.com launches on 1 Junem 2018. Sign-up now for updates.

Little White Lies

TRUTH & MOVIES

10%
DISCOUNT

———

Get 5 issues for as little as £22*
with the code LWL75

———

To subscribe, head to lwlies.imbmsubscriptions.com
Or call us on +44 (0)1293 312096

*Discount off full subscription cost of £33 for 6 issues.
Delivered over 14 months. Applied at checkout.

ROOFTOP
FILM CLUB

Little White Lies

Published by TCO
Little White Lies – Huck - 71a

Words, pictures, thanks... Lenny Abrahamson, Mark Adams, Babak Anvari, Mark Asch, Roca Balboa, JA Bayona, Abby Bender, Diego Cadena Bejarano, Anton Bitel, Edith Bowman, Charles Bramesco, Holly Brockwell, Efe Cakarel, Michelle Carey, Jaime Christley, Phil Concannon, Stephen Cone, Laia Costa, Adam Lee Davies, Guillermo Del Toro, Hope Dickson Leach, Ella Donald, Allison Filice, Filippo Fontana, Emma Fraser, Marya E Gates, Caroline Golum, Glenn Heath Jr., Thomas Hobbs, Tom Huddleston, Pamela Hutchinson, Eve Jones, Timothy George Kelly, Brodie Lancaster, Joe Lawlor, Elena Lazic, Manuela Lazic, Michael Leader, Guy Lodge, Kim Longinotto, James Luxford, Christine Malloy, Alicia Malone, Ian Mantgani, Penny Martin, Mike McCahill, Katherine McLaughlin, Tuppence Middleton, Sophie Monks Kaufman, Adam Nayman, Jarod Neece, Christina Newland, Jason Ngai, Ben Nicholson, Charlie Phillips, Gina Prince-Blythewood, Pepa Prieto Puy, Laurie Rose, Benny Safdie, Josh Safdie, Carol Salter, Roxanne Sancto, Michael Sheen, Josh Slater-Williams, Michael Smiley, Justine Smith, Matt Thrift, Colin Trevorrow, Matt Turner, Eve Watling Beth Webb

Editorial

Editor
David Jenkins
david@tcolondon.com

Digital Editor
Adam Woodward
adam@tcolondon.com

Social Producer
Hannah Woodhead
hannah@tcolondon.com

Contributing Editor
Sophie Monks Kaufman
sophie@tcolondon.com

Interns
Eve Jones
Malika Kingston

Art

Art Director - LWLies
Laurene Boglio
laurene@tcolondon.com

Art Director – Huck
Oliver Stafford
oliver
@tcolondon.com

Graphic Designer
Sophie Mo
sophie.mo
@tcolondon.com

Graphic Designer
Simon Hayes
simon.hayes
@tcolondon.com

TCO - Agency

Managing Director
Simon Baker
simon@tcolondon.com

Executive Producer
Steven Farah
steven@tcolondon.com

Head of Strategy
D'Arcy Doran
darcy@tcolondon.com

Head of Creative Studio
Rachel Goldsworthy
rachel@tcolondon.com

Editorial Lead
Michael Fordham
michael@tcolondon.com

Branded Books
Clive Wilson
clive@tcolondon.com

71A Gallery

Studio Manager
Jon Denham
jon@tcolondon.com

Publishing

Publisher
Vince Medeiros
vince@tcolondon.com

Head of Partnerships
Chris DeHaney
chris@tcolondon.com

Media Sales
Oliver Slade
oliver.slade
@tcolondon.com

Special Projects
Steph Pomphrey
steph@tcolondon.com

Legal
Alex Wade

General Manager
Wendy Klerck
wendy@tcolondon.com

Cover Artwork
Adam Hayes
mrahayes.com

The articles appearing in this publication reflect the opinions of their respective authors and not necessarily those of the publishers or editorial team.

TCOLondon 2018
(copyright)

Published by
TCO Publishing
71a Leonard Street
London EC2A 4QS UK
+44 (0) 207-729-3675
tcolondon.com
info@tcolondon.com

LWLies is published
5 times a year

Advertise in LWLies
Oliver Slade
oliver.slade
@tcolondon.com
+44 (0) 207-729-3675

Stock LWLies
Circulation Marketing
& Distribution
Intermedia Brand
Marketing Ltd.
getintouch
@inter-media.co.uk
01293 312110

Specialist Distribution
MMS Ltd
Info@mmslondon.co.uk
01992 676064

Printed by Buxton Press

Lwlies.com

Film that resonates ...

barbican

Sun 13 May
Waltz with Bashir
with Max Richter's score
performed live by
Chineke! Orchestra

Wed 16 May
Salomé
with new score by Haley Fohr
of Circuit des Yeux

Sat 1 Dec
Last and First Men
with Jóhann Jóhannsson's score live

CITY
OF
LONDON

The City of London
Corporation is the founder
and principal funder
of the Barbican Centre